On My Knees ... For These

WestBow Press books may be ordered through booksellers or by contacting:

WestBow Press
A Division of Thomas Nelson
1663 Liberty Drive
Bloomington, IN 47403
www.westbowpress.com
1-(866) 928-1240

Due to the dynamic nature of the Internet, any web
addresses or links contained in this book may have changed
since publication and may no longer be valid.

The views expressed in this work are solely those of the author
and do not necessarily reflect the views of the publisher, and the
publisher hereby disclaims any responsibility for them.

All "Journal Entries" and "Inspirational Quotes"
included in this book were written solely by the author.

Library of Congress Control Number: 2011963343

ISBN: 978-1-4497-3549-4 (sc)

Printed in the United States of America

WestBow Press rev. date:1/11/2012

On My Knees ...
For These

A 52-week Journey
of Prayer & Intercession

Written By
Mary Charlotte Barry

"For the Lord takes delight in His people;
He crowns the humble with salvation.
Let the saints rejoice in His honor
and sing for joy on their beds."
Psalm 149:4-5 (NIV®)

Presented To

_____

_____

By

_____

_____

Date

_____

"My mouth will speak in praise of the Lord.
Let every creature praise His holy name
forever and ever"
Psalm 145:21 (NIV®)

FOREWORD

I love this book because it has the potential of being such a powerful blessing to people just like me who struggle with prayer. Though I have been pastoring for over 25 years, I continue to find myself challenged in the place of intercession. If you're like me, you will find many encouragements within these pages to help you become more focused and directed in your time with the Lord.

As you read Mary's simple, yet faith-filled approach to meeting with God, I know you will be challenged to apply your faith with a broader brush.

Paul D. LeBoutillier

Paul D. LeBoutillier, Senior Pastor
Calvary Chapel
Ontario, OR
www.ccontario.com

*"Trust in the Lord with all your heart
and lean not on your own understanding;
in all your ways acknowledge Him,
and He will make your paths straight."*

Proverbs 3:5-6 (NIV®)

Life's purpose...

To know Him
To love Him
To serve Him
To share Him

Table of Contents

"Praise the Lord.
Praise the Lord, O my soul.
I will praise the Lord all my life;
I will sing praise to my God as long as I live."
Psalm 146:1-2 (NIV®)

DEDICATION

My first love is my Lord and Savior and He has graciously blessed me with my second love ... my family. I have been married to my husband and soul mate, Robert, for nearly forty-two years. We have two beautiful and talented daughters and, together, we have shared in the delights and blessings fashioned by seven amazing grandchildren. I am blessed with years of wonderful memories, life encounters, and joy unimaginable from God's most precious and generous gifts.

To Mom and Daddy,
Thank you for your constant love and encouragement.
You will always be forever in my heart.

To my husband, Robert,
Always giving his everlasting love and encouragement;
To my daughters, Christen and Amanda,
As my inspiration and constantly exhibiting their faith in me;
To our beautiful grandchildren
Who bring joy and laughter to my life;

But, most importantly, our Lord and Savior ... for all of the above!

And ... as will always be—

"I can do all things through Christ Who strengthens me."
Philippians 4:13 (NIV®)

"You are the light of the world.
A city on a hill cannot be hidden.
Neither do people light a lamp
And put it under a bowl.
Instead, they put it on its stand,
And it gives light to everyone in the house.
In the same way, let your light shine before men,
That they may see your good deeds
And praise your Father in heaven."
Matthew 5:14-16

GUIDING US HOME

From the time our daughters were pre-teens, we spent our annual vacations in Yachats (pronounced Ya-hots), a sleepy little retirement town on the Oregon Coast. Even now, my husband and I still choose to spend our vacation getaways there. We have witnessed the most magnificent illustrations of God's handiwork: a radiant sun descending below the horizon cascading ribbons of color across the ocean's surface; the moon glistening in the stillness, reflecting on the waters below; and the same sun rising over the eastern mountains to start this unbelievable scene all over again, but one particular site truly renews my spirit. A few miles up the coastline, there is a lighthouse that stands majestically at the cliff's edge. We have all learned its purpose is to steer mariners, while in dense fog or dark nights, away from cliffs, land, and coral reefs. It provides a signal to ships to avoid a perilous situation. The ship's crew trusts the keeper of the light to guide them safely home.

As with the lighthouse, our heavenly Father provides the Light which guides us to a safe harbor. He offers us the opportunity to steer our lives in a direction that will keep us out of harm's way, with His lead. The lighthouse may be manmade, but as Christians, its objective is easily paralleled with Christ's purpose in our lives. He is our Light and our Hope for a safe journey home.

"I have come into the world as a light,
so that no one who believes in Me shall stay in darkness."
John 12:46 (NIV®)

DATE _____ PRAYER NEED _____
_____

DATE _____ PRAYER NEED _____
_____

DATE _____ PRAYER NEED _____
_____

DATE _____ PRAYER NEED _____
_____

DATE _____ PRAYER NEED _____
_____

DATE _____ PRAYER NEED _____
_____

DATE _____ PRAYER NEED _____
_____

DATE _____ PRAYER NEED _____
_____

DATE _____ PRAYER NEED _____
_____

DATE _____ PRAYER NEED _____
_____

DATE _____ PRAYER NEED _____

_____

_____

DATE _____ PRAYER NEED _____

_____

_____

DATE _____ PRAYER NEED _____

_____

_____

DATE _____ PRAYER NEED _____

_____

_____

DATE _____ PRAYER NEED _____

_____

_____

DATE _____ PRAYER NEED _____

_____

_____

DATE _____ PRAYER NEED _____

_____

_____

DATE _____ PRAYER NEED _____

_____

_____

"I will lead the blind by ways they have not known,
along unfamiliar paths I will guide them;
I will turn the darkness into light before them
and make the rough places smooth"
Isaiah 42:16 (NIV ®)

DATE _____ PRAYER NEED _____

_____

DATE _____ PRAYER NEED _____

_____

DATE _____ PRAYER NEED _____

_____

DATE _____ PRAYER NEED _____

_____

NOTES

_____

_____

_____

_____

_____

_____

_____

_____

_____

_____

_____

CAUSE AND EFFECT

My days become engulfed with my writing, my family and responsibilities in our home, making moments with Him very valuable and precious. "Time" can be defined as an instance, a moment or an hour, but in reality "time" is invaluable to all of us. I look forward each morning to sitting at my keyboard, writing personal stories, expressing emotions, and sharing memorable experiences.

Although I make every effort to converse with Him throughout my day, I know that the individual prayers I send upwards are the most valuable gifts I may offer. I will likely never know the consequences of my prayers as they trickle out like a pebble tossed in a pond. Circle after circle spreads further and further out to a point unrecognizable; as one prayer may lead to another and then to another and so on. I may not see the end result, but only the rippling effect in the beginning. Someday, He may reveal the answers to me. For now, I am content to simply be the pebble.

"He has made everything beautiful in its time.
He has also set eternity in the hearts of men;
yet they cannot fathom what God has done
from beginning to end."
Ecclesiastes 3:11 (NIV R)

DATE _____ PRAYER NEED _____
_____

DATE _____ PRAYER NEED _____
_____

DATE _____ PRAYER NEED _____
_____

DATE _____ PRAYER NEED _____
_____

DATE _____ PRAYER NEED _____
_____

DATE _____ PRAYER NEED _____
_____

DATE _____ PRAYER NEED _____
_____

DATE _____ PRAYER NEED _____
_____

DATE _____ PRAYER NEED _____
_____

DATE _____ PRAYER NEED _____
_____

DATE _____ PRAYER NEED _____

_____

DATE _____ PRAYER NEED _____

_____

DATE _____ PRAYER NEED _____

_____

DATE _____ PRAYER NEED _____

_____

DATE _____ PRAYER NEED _____

_____

DATE _____ PRAYER NEED _____

_____

DATE _____ PRAYER NEED _____

_____

DATE _____ PRAYER NEED _____

_____

"I wait for You, O Lord; You will answer,
O Lord my God."
Psalm 38:15 (NIV/R)

DATE _____ PRAYER NEED _____

_____

_____

DATE _____ PRAYER NEED _____

_____

_____

DATE _____ PRAYER NEED _____

_____

_____

DATE _____ PRAYER NEED _____

_____

_____

NOTES

_____

_____

_____

_____

_____

_____

_____

_____

_____

_____

_____

_____

COMMANDING HIS ATTENTION

I am blessed to be the grandmother of the most amazing grandchildren. They each show us a distinct and individual spirit with a loving heart overflowing with desires, interests and ambitions that are often at opposite ends of the spectrum. Whether the girls or the boys, they all have the same adoring love for their grandpa. From the toddlers to the teens, they all find their own way to command his attention. Crawling up on his lap, snuggling side-by-side or by simply having a heartfelt conversation; they never ignore his presence.

Isn't this as it should be with our heavenly Father? Command His attention, strike up a conversation in prayer or snuggle up to His comforting and adoring Spirit. We may choose the method, but be assured, He will ALWAYS respond.

"... Ascribe to the Lord the glory due His name.
Bring an offering and come before Him;
worship the Lord in the splendor of His holiness."
1 Chronicles 16:29 (NIV®)

DATE _____ PRAYER NEED _____
_____

DATE _____ PRAYER NEED _____
_____

DATE _____ PRAYER NEED _____
_____

DATE _____ PRAYER NEED _____
_____

DATE _____ PRAYER NEED _____
_____

DATE _____ PRAYER NEED _____
_____

DATE _____ PRAYER NEED _____
_____

DATE _____ PRAYER NEED _____
_____

DATE _____ PRAYER NEED _____
_____

DATE _____ PRAYER NEED _____
_____

DATE _____ PRAYER NEED _____

_____

DATE _____ PRAYER NEED _____

_____

DATE _____ PRAYER NEED _____

_____

DATE _____ PRAYER NEED _____

_____

DATE _____ PRAYER NEED _____

_____

DATE _____ PRAYER NEED _____

_____

DATE _____ PRAYER NEED _____

_____

DATE _____ PRAYER NEED _____

_____

"It is written in the Prophets,
they will all be taught by God.
Everyone who listens to the Father
and learns from Him comes to Me."
John 6:45 (NIV®)

DATE _____ PRAYER NEED _____
_____
_____

DATE _____ PRAYER NEED _____
_____
_____

DATE _____ PRAYER NEED _____
_____
_____

DATE _____ PRAYER NEED _____
_____
_____

NOTES

_____
_____
_____
_____
_____
_____
_____
_____
_____
_____
_____
_____

PRAYERFUL FOCUS

Today, there were no prayer requests through our church mail group, which was uplifting, but also a bit discouraging. There is that place within me that delights in knowing I fill an essential position with regard to the prayerful needs of others; in whatever capacity. Don't get me wrong, receiving praise reports is very encouraging; however, today I found myself starring at an empty inbox. It was at that moment I heard a familiar sound; the hum of my neighbors riding mower. I glanced out the office window to see Leah, 82 years young, performing her weekly ritual since the loss of her husband several years earlier.

Then it occurred to me, I am finding myself focusing only on the prayer needs of my church family via e-mail, when I should be looking outward, as well; to my own family, my neighbors, distant friends; whether simple or complex; a prayer for comfort or illness; prayer for finances or protection; or simply a prayer for a sweet, elderly neighbor who fills her lonely days with menial tasks. Leah would be the focus of my prayers today.

"Therefore, as God's chosen people, holy and dearly loved,
clothe yourselves with compassion, kindness,
humility, gentleness and patience"
Colossians 3:12 (NIV ®)

DATE _____ PRAYER NEED _____

_____

DATE _____ PRAYER NEED _____

_____

DATE _____ PRAYER NEED _____

_____

DATE _____ PRAYER NEED _____

_____

DATE _____ PRAYER NEED _____

_____

DATE _____ PRAYER NEED _____

_____

DATE _____ PRAYER NEED _____

_____

DATE _____ PRAYER NEED _____

_____

DATE _____ PRAYER NEED _____

_____

DATE _____ PRAYER NEED _____

_____

DATE _____ PRAYER NEED _____
_____
_____

DATE _____ PRAYER NEED _____
_____
_____

DATE _____ PRAYER NEED _____
_____
_____

DATE _____ PRAYER NEED _____
_____
_____

DATE _____ PRAYER NEED _____
_____
_____

DATE _____ PRAYER NEED _____
_____
_____

DATE _____ PRAYER NEED _____
_____
_____

DATE _____ PRAYER NEED _____
_____
_____

"Be devoted to one another in brotherly love.
Honor one another above yourselves"
Romans 12:10 (NIV®)

DATE _____ PRAYER NEED _____
_____
_____

DATE _____ PRAYER NEED _____
_____
_____

DATE _____ PRAYER NEED _____
_____
_____

DATE _____ PRAYER NEED _____
_____
_____

NOTES

_____
_____
_____
_____
_____
_____
_____
_____
_____
_____
_____
_____

A Time for Fresh Faith †

Each day we drop to our knees, clutch our hands together, close our eyes and speak to the Father. We kneel before Him on behalf of another; a loved one, a friend, or perhaps an individual we may never meet. When we bear the heart of a prayer warrior, we must be focused; our minds clear of distraction and our surroundings calm. Today, I ask you to say aloud, "I am on my knees for me."

The day has come to take a breath; time to replenish; time to request a spiritual "tune-up." This is not a selfish act, but a desperately needed one. Asking Him for the needs in your own life is necessary to keep your mind clear of worries and concerns and offers you the ability to be faithful with your commitment to pray for others. Petition the Lord for yourself. Start by asking Him for a refreshing of your spirit.

On the reverse of this page, list the areas in your own life where you desire His help; whether financial, physical, spiritual, or emotional. Be willing to remove your shoes and lay face down before Him. He adores you and wants your desires to become His. Open your heart, call out His name and allow Him to offer "Fresh Faith."

"Delight yourself in the Lord
and He will give you the desires of your heart.
Commit your way to the Lord; trust in Him and He will do this:
He will make your righteousness shine like the dawn,
the justice of your cause like the noonday sun."
Psalms 37:4-6 (NIV ®)

MY PRAYER, MY NEEDS_____

_____

_____

_____

_____

_____

_____

_____

_____

_____

_____

_____

_____

_____

_____

"Do not be anxious about anything, but in everything,
by prayer and petition, with thanksgiving,
present your requests to God .
And the peace of God, which transcends all understanding,
will guard your hearts and your minds in Christ Jesus."
Philippians 4:6-7 (NIV®)

Our Childlike Ways

Both my girls are in their thirties now with children of their own; but I cannot give a single thought to what my life would have been without them. They are nothing alike in physical appearance, personality or life goals ... but, they both have a tender and open heart to the Father. They are guiding their own children in the same direction, giving them gentle nudges along the way.

As children and as adults, prayer has never been a time to be timid, but an opportunity to bring our needs to the Lord. Remembering, as a child, it was as any other conversation; casually and trustingly addressing Him as though speaking to a teacher or a friend. There was no doubt in our mind that He was listening. As adults, we should take a lesson from our children. Come to the Lord "BELIEVING," confident that He hears our petitions.

"Therefore I tell you, whatever you ask for in prayer,
BELIEVE that you have received it, and it will be yours."

Mark 11:24 (NIV®)

Date _____ Prayer Need _____

_____

Date _____ Prayer Need _____

_____

Date _____ Prayer Need _____

_____

Date _____ Prayer Need _____

_____

Date _____ Prayer Need _____

_____

Date _____ Prayer Need _____

_____

Date _____ Prayer Need _____

_____

Date _____ Prayer Need _____

_____

Date _____ Prayer Need _____

_____

Date _____ Prayer Need _____

_____

DATE _____ PRAYER NEED _____
_____
_____

DATE _____ PRAYER NEED _____
_____
_____

DATE _____ PRAYER NEED _____
_____
_____

DATE _____ PRAYER NEED _____
_____
_____

DATE _____ PRAYER NEED _____
_____
_____

DATE _____ PRAYER NEED _____
_____
_____

DATE _____ PRAYER NEED _____
_____
_____

DATE _____ PRAYER NEED _____
_____
_____

*"Now to Him who is able to do immeasurably more
than all we ask or imagine,
according to His power that is at work within us."*
Ephesians 3:20 (NIV®)

DATE _____ PRAYER NEED_____

_____

DATE _____ PRAYER NEED_____

_____

DATE _____ PRAYER NEED_____

_____

DATE _____ PRAYER NEED_____

_____

NOTES

_____

_____

_____

_____

_____

_____

_____

_____

_____

_____

_____

LETTING GO

On a chilly October morning, my sweet mom chose heaven over earth. She said good-bye to Dad seven years earlier, but nothing could fill the void he left behind and she longed to be with him again. My sister and I stayed by her bedside for ten days, watching, as she slowly slipped away. It wasn't until our brother drove a 1,000 miles to say good-bye that she finally reached out her hand to the Father and He walked her through the gates of Heaven and into Dad's awaiting arms.

Although her gentle spirit helps to fill the emptiness, my heart aches for her adoring hugs and kisses. Even weeks after her passing, there were days when the scent of her sweet perfume would fill my office and my mind would wander to distant memories and the tears would not stop. It would have been overwhelming, had I allowed myself to become engulfed by grief and helplessness, but if I continued to stretch out my hand to another, knowing that my Father in Heaven was stretching out His hand to me; calm enveloped me for which I found no explanation. His constant presence was and is the assurance that I will see her again in a heavenly place. I will continue to pray for another's needs, as He continues to comfort me through my own.

"He died for us so that, whether we are awake or asleep,
we may live together with Him"
1 Thessalonians 5:10 (NIV®)

DATE _____ PRAYER NEED _____
_____

DATE _____ PRAYER NEED _____
_____

DATE _____ PRAYER NEED _____
_____

DATE _____ PRAYER NEED _____
_____

DATE _____ PRAYER NEED _____
_____

DATE _____ PRAYER NEED _____
_____

DATE _____ PRAYER NEED _____
_____

DATE _____ PRAYER NEED _____
_____

DATE _____ PRAYER NEED _____
_____

DATE _____ PRAYER NEED _____
_____

DATE _____ PRAYER NEED _____
_____
_____

DATE _____ PRAYER NEED _____
_____
_____

DATE _____ PRAYER NEED _____
_____
_____

DATE _____ PRAYER NEED _____
_____
_____

DATE _____ PRAYER NEED _____
_____
_____

DATE _____ PRAYER NEED _____
_____
_____

DATE _____ PRAYER NEED _____
_____
_____

DATE _____ PRAYER NEED _____
_____
_____

"Even though I walk through the valley
of the shadow of death,
I will fear no evil, for You are with me;
Your rod and Your staff, they comfort me."
Psalm 23:4 (NIV®)

Date _____ Prayer Need _____

_____

Date _____ Prayer Need _____

_____

Date _____ Prayer Need _____

_____

Date _____ Prayer Need _____

_____

Notes

_____

_____

_____

_____

_____

_____

_____

_____

_____

_____

_____

EARTHLY HEROES

My dad was committed to his family, labored in several professions, taught his children respect for others and was well admired by his peers. He also adored his grandchildren and gladly dished out lots of teasing, followed by a generous portion of hugs. I was the only one of the siblings that called him "Daddy." I can still close my eyes and breathe in the scent of his favorite cigar and his after shave. He and mom met on a blind date, but were soul mates from the start; drifting off to sleep every night; hand-in-hand. Alzheimer's didn't just draw the life out of Dad, it drained his spirit. The day we placed him in the care center was a painful experience for all of us, but Dad would have moments of clarity. A few days prior, he reached out his hand to mom and told her, softly, "Peggy, you have to do what you have to do … it's okay," then his mind would retreat to that place unreachable, once again.

Daddy made his journey to the Kingdom, a few short weeks later and four months after celebrating their fifty-sixth wedding anniversary. His earthly life ended more than eleven years ago, but his bright smile, sense of humor and playful spirit will always be with us.

"Jesus answered him, 'I tell you the truth,
today you will be with Me in paradise.'"

Luke 23:43 (NIV ®)

DATE _____ PRAYER NEED _____
_____

DATE _____ PRAYER NEED _____
_____

DATE _____ PRAYER NEED _____
_____

DATE _____ PRAYER NEED _____
_____

DATE _____ PRAYER NEED _____
_____

DATE _____ PRAYER NEED _____
_____

DATE _____ PRAYER NEED _____
_____

DATE _____ PRAYER NEED _____
_____

DATE _____ PRAYER NEED _____
_____

DATE _____ PRAYER NEED _____
_____

DATE _____ PRAYER NEED _____

_____

DATE _____ PRAYER NEED _____

_____

DATE _____ PRAYER NEED _____

_____

DATE _____ PRAYER NEED _____

_____

DATE _____ PRAYER NEED _____

_____

DATE _____ PRAYER NEED _____

_____

DATE _____ PRAYER NEED _____

_____

DATE _____ PRAYER NEED _____

_____

*"Now there is in store for me the crown of righteousness,
which the Lord, the righteous Judge,
will award to me on that day—and not only to me,
but also to all who have longed for His appearing."
II Timothy 4:8 (NIV ®)*

Date _____ Prayer Need _____
_____
_____

Date _____ Prayer Need _____
_____
_____

Date _____ Prayer Need _____
_____
_____

Date _____ Prayer Need _____
_____
_____

Notes

_____
_____
_____
_____
_____
_____
_____
_____
_____
_____
_____
_____

RE-GIFTING

God daily reveals evidence that the Holy Spirit is at work in my life. First, I testify that Jesus is Savior; second, I rely on the love that God will never take away; third, I believe that I am created in His image; and lastly, I must believe that I love, because He first loved me. The Holy Spirit is persistently prodding me to share my faith and encourage others through my actions and my words and I can do so by "living my faith out loud". Recalling my Sunday school classes and the song, "This Little Light of Mine", I am reminded of the hand gestures, cupping one hand over the other, for the stanza, "Hide it under a bushel, no! I'm gonna let it shine!"

Sharing these evidences with others, allows me to "shine". Whether by holding a hand in prayer or offering encouragement through hardship, His love is the one gift that we are permitted to re-wrap and pass on to another.

"I long to see you,
so that I may impart to you some spiritual gift
to make you strong—that is,
that you and I may be mutually encouraged by each other's faith."
Romans 1:11-12 (NIV®)

DATE _____ PRAYER NEED _____
_____

DATE _____ PRAYER NEED _____
_____

DATE _____ PRAYER NEED _____
_____

DATE _____ PRAYER NEED _____
_____

DATE _____ PRAYER NEED _____
_____

DATE _____ PRAYER NEED _____
_____

DATE _____ PRAYER NEED _____
_____

DATE _____ PRAYER NEED _____
_____

DATE _____ PRAYER NEED _____
_____

DATE _____ PRAYER NEED _____
_____

DATE _____PRAYER NEED_____

_____

_____

DATE _____PRAYER NEED_____

_____

_____

DATE _____PRAYER NEED_____

_____

DATE _____PRAYER NEED_____

_____

DATE _____PRAYER NEED_____

_____

DATE _____PRAYER NEED_____

_____

DATE _____PRAYER NEED_____

_____

DATE _____PRAYER NEED_____

_____

_____

*"Now faith is being sure of what we hope for
and certain of what we do not see."*
Hebrews 11:1 (NIV®)

Date _____ PRAYER NEED_____

_____

_____

Date _____ PRAYER NEED_____

_____

_____

Date _____ PRAYER NEED_____

_____

_____

Date _____ PRAYER NEED_____

_____

_____

NOTES

_____

_____

_____

_____

_____

_____

_____

_____

_____

_____

_____

A Time for Fresh Faith †

Once again, the day has come to say, "I am on my knees for me." Time to take a breath; time to replenish your spiritual strength; time to seek His guidance and to petition the Lord for yourself; time to ask Him for a refreshing of your spirit.

On the reverse of this page, list the areas in your own life where you desire His help; financial, physical, spiritual, or emotional.

Be willing to remove your shoes and lay face down before Him. He adores you and wants your desires to become His.

Open your heart, call out His name …
Allow Him to offer "Fresh Faith."

"Delight yourself in the Lord
and He will give you the desires of your heart.
Commit your way to the Lord; trust in Him and He will do this:
He will make your righteousness shine like the dawn.
the justice of your cause like the noonday sun."
Psalms 37:4-6 (NIV®)

MY PRAYER, MY NEEDS

_"Do not be anxious about anything, but in everything,
by prayer and petition, with thanksgiving,
present your requests to God .
And the peace of God, which transcends all understanding,
will guard your hearts and your minds in Christ Jesus."
Philippians 4:6-7_ (NIV®)

Unseen Gifts

At the age of three, my cousin's little boy was diagnosed with cancer (Stage III Hepatoblastoma). He endured this horrifying disease for eighteen months before taking the hand of Jesus; leaving his suffering behind. God's gift of this beautiful child encircled us all in a way that we cannot define. We may not feel that the miracle we had been praying for had come to fulfillment, but, you see, through the love and compassion of the Father … this little one touched more individuals, opened more hearts and created more joy than we would ever have felt possible in his four and a half years with us. Regardless of the outcome, his family and all those who continued to pray for him, were the recipients of unseen gifts that will manifest themselves for years to come. He is whole in Christ, so, you see, our prayers for healing *were* answered.

Though we seek the Father, wanting desperately to believe, our flesh brings forth that tiny shred of doubt … deep down, as we attempt to hide from His face. Doubting whether He sees our pain; doubting if He hears our pleas; doubting His will. He knows. He sees the tears we shed with each drop to our knees. He hears our cries when we become frightened or angry. He knows, as well, that we still love Him; we still trust Him; we will still seek Him; no matter the outcome.

(Visit www.bumblebeefoundation.org)

"Jesus said, 'Let the little children come to Me,
and do not hinder them,
for the Kingdom of Heaven belongs to such as these.'"
Matthew 19:14 (NIV ®)

Date _____ Prayer Need _____

_____

Date _____ Prayer Need _____

_____

Date _____ Prayer Need _____

_____

Date _____ Prayer Need _____

_____

Date _____ Prayer Need _____

_____

Date _____ Prayer Need _____

_____

Date _____ Prayer Need _____

_____

Date _____ Prayer Need _____

_____

Date _____ Prayer Need _____

_____

Date _____ Prayer Need _____

_____

DATE _____ PRAYER NEED _____
_____
_____

DATE _____ PRAYER NEED _____
_____
_____

DATE _____ PRAYER NEED _____
_____
_____

DATE _____ PRAYER NEED _____
_____
_____

DATE _____ PRAYER NEED _____
_____
_____

DATE _____ PRAYER NEED _____
_____
_____

DATE _____ PRAYER NEED _____
_____
_____

DATE _____ PRAYER NEED _____
_____
_____

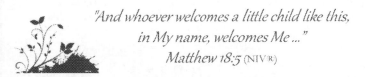

"And whoever welcomes a little child like this,
in My name, welcomes Me ..."
Matthew 18:5 (NIV/R)

DATE _____ PRAYER NEED _____
_____
_____

DATE _____ PRAYER NEED _____
_____
_____

DATE _____ PRAYER NEED _____
_____
_____

DATE _____ PRAYER NEED _____
_____
_____

NOTES

_____
_____
_____
_____
_____
_____
_____
_____
_____
_____
_____

I Cannot Do it Alone

I hand it to Him … I take it back … again and again … it is exhausting, but it is within my own human nature to attempt to solve my problems myself. There is a defining moment when I clearly see His face and experience the realization that I can do nothing else, but that I must give it up to Him. Although the love of my Heavenly Father is greater than my own earthly mind could possibly comprehend, as a believer, I do know that His love is everlasting and has the ability to carry me through the gravest of circumstances. My imagination, as vivid as it may be, is completely unable to conjure up any other possible solution. We have no alternate course to take except to continue a futile attempt to fix something that we have no business tinkering with alone.

Remember this … if you choose to "go it alone", take that statement literally. It is much more gratifying when you can finally admit that you work best with a partner; a partner who will watch your back! He is a partner who is trusting, a partner who is loyal, a partner who is faithful, and a partner who will never leave you or forsake you.

*"May your unfailing love rest upon us,
O Lord, even as we put our hope in You."*
Psalm 33:22 (NIV®)

DATE _____ PRAYER NEED _____
_____

DATE _____ PRAYER NEED _____
_____

DATE _____ PRAYER NEED _____
_____

DATE _____ PRAYER NEED _____
_____

DATE _____ PRAYER NEED _____
_____

DATE _____ PRAYER NEED _____
_____

DATE _____ PRAYER NEED _____
_____

DATE _____ PRAYER NEED _____
_____

DATE _____ PRAYER NEED _____
_____

DATE _____ PRAYER NEED _____
_____

DATE _____PRAYER NEED_____

_____

DATE _____PRAYER NEED_____

_____

DATE _____PRAYER NEED_____

_____

DATE _____PRAYER NEED_____

_____

DATE _____PRAYER NEED_____

_____

DATE _____PRAYER NEED_____

_____

DATE _____PRAYER NEED_____

_____

DATE _____PRAYER NEED_____

_____

_____

"Then they believed His promises
and sang His praise."
Psalm 106:12 (NIV R)

Date _____ Prayer Need _____
_____

Date _____ Prayer Need _____
_____

Date _____ Prayer Need _____
_____

Date _____ Prayer Need _____
_____

Notes

_____
_____
_____
_____
_____
_____
_____
_____
_____
_____
_____

LIVING ANEW

On Sunday, January 19, 1975, during an impromptu gathering at our home, my husband and I made a personal commitment to our Lord and Savior. We opened our hearts and He opened our eyes to a new beginning and a new life. Since that day, we have faced physical, financial, emotional and spiritual changes in our lives; each time, clutching to our faith and to His grace. As a Christian, I can boldly say, the decision to open my heart and asking Christ to occupy that once empty space is an event that will not be surpassed until that day when He calls me home and I stand before His throne.

Father God … I lift my hands to you as I give you praise and glory for your unconditional love and amazing power that allows me to continue in this journey. My life is filled with hope and strength that can only be acquired by walking with you. You are my awesome God; my Rescuer; my Savior.

"For God so loved the world
that He gave His one and only Son,
that whoever believes in Him
shall not perish, but have eternal life."
John 3:16 (NIV®)

DATE _____ PRAYER NEED _____
_____

DATE _____ PRAYER NEED _____
_____

DATE _____ PRAYER NEED _____
_____

DATE _____ PRAYER NEED _____
_____

DATE _____ PRAYER NEED _____
_____

DATE _____ PRAYER NEED _____
_____

DATE _____ PRAYER NEED _____
_____

DATE _____ PRAYER NEED _____
_____

DATE _____ PRAYER NEED _____
_____

DATE _____ PRAYER NEED _____
_____

DATE _____ PRAYER NEED _____

_____

_____

DATE _____ PRAYER NEED _____

_____

_____

DATE _____ PRAYER NEED _____

_____

_____

DATE _____ PRAYER NEED _____

_____

_____

DATE _____ PRAYER NEED _____

_____

_____

DATE _____ PRAYER NEED _____

_____

_____

DATE _____ PRAYER NEED _____

_____

_____

DATE _____ PRAYER NEED _____

_____

_____

"Here I am! I stand at the door and knock.
If anyone hears My voice and opens the door,
I will go in and eat with him and he with Me."
Revelation 3:20 (NIV®)

DATE _____ PRAYER NEED _____

_____

_____

DATE _____ PRAYER NEED _____

_____

_____

DATE _____ PRAYER NEED _____

_____

_____

DATE _____ PRAYER NEED _____

_____

_____

NOTES

_____

_____

_____

_____

_____

_____

_____

_____

_____

_____

_____

_____

CHILDHOOD LESSONS

God invites me into His presence without hesitation and without judgment. It is within me to choose to either spend quality time with Him or to ignore His calling. Yet, He adores His children and chooses to love me regardless of my indiscretions. On those days, I reach deep within myself, all the way to my toes. It is also on those days that I can clearly hear my mother's words, "Mary Charlotte, this furniture cannot dust itself!" We shared the chores and dusting was mine. Funny … at five, it was fun, by the time I reached my teens, it was anything but fun. It took up my free time, my phone time and my friend time, but it was my responsibility. It was this discipline that assisted in teaching me the importance of doing for others and in turn, praying for others. Now, time in prayer is time I embrace.

It is His love, His grace and His promise that brings me to my knees each day in obedience. Let's not allow dust to accumulate at the altar.

"In Him and through faith in Him,
we may approach God with freedom and confidence."
Ephesians 3:12 (NIV R)

Date _____ Prayer Need _____
_____

Date _____ Prayer Need _____
_____

Date _____ Prayer Need _____
_____

Date _____ Prayer Need _____
_____

Date _____ Prayer Need _____
_____

Date _____ Prayer Need _____
_____

Date _____ Prayer Need _____
_____

Date _____ Prayer Need _____
_____

Date _____ Prayer Need _____
_____

Date _____ Prayer Need _____
_____

DATE _____ PRAYER NEED _____

_____

_____

DATE _____ PRAYER NEED _____

_____

_____

DATE _____ PRAYER NEED _____

_____

_____

DATE _____ PRAYER NEED _____

_____

_____

DATE _____ PRAYER NEED _____

_____

_____

DATE _____ PRAYER NEED _____

_____

_____

DATE _____ PRAYER NEED _____

_____

_____

DATE _____ PRAYER NEED _____

_____

_____

"Therefore, strengthen your feeble arms and weak knees.
Make level paths for your feet,
so that the lame may not be disabled,
but rather healed."
Hebrews 12:12-13 (NIV®)

DATE _____ PRAYER NEED _____

_____

DATE _____ PRAYER NEED _____

_____

DATE _____ PRAYER NEED _____

_____

DATE _____ PRAYER NEED _____

_____

NOTES

_____

_____

_____

_____

_____

_____

_____

_____

_____

_____

_____

A Time for Fresh Faith †

Once again, the day has come to say, "I am on my knees for me." Time to take a breath; time to replenish your spiritual strength; time to seek His guidance and to petition the Lord for yourself; time to ask Him for a refreshing of your spirit.

On the reverse of this page, list the areas in your own life where you desire His help; financial, physical, spiritual, or emotional.

Be willing to remove your shoes and lay face down before Him. He adores you and wants your desires to become His.

Open your heart, call out His name …
Allow Him to offer "Fresh Faith."

"Delight yourself in the Lord
and He will give you the desires of your heart.
Commit your way to the Lord; trust in Him and He will do this:
He will make your righteousness shine like the dawn,
the justice of your cause like the noonday sun."
Psalms 37:4-6 (NIV®)

MY PRAYER, MY NEEDS

_____

_____

_____

_____

_____

_____

_____

_____

_____

_____

_____

_____

_____

_____

_____

_____

_____

_____

_____

_____

_____

_____

"Do not be anxious about anything, but in everything,
by prayer and petition, with thanksgiving,
present your requests to God .
And the peace of God, which transcends all understanding,
will guard your hearts and your minds in Christ Jesus."
Philippians 4:6-7 (NIV®)

CHOSEN TO SERVE

So often it feels as though I am repeating the same prayer over and over and over, but whatever the reason, I must remember … I was chosen for this journey, no matter how monotonous it may seem. I never want to feel as though I am resting on my heels allowing someone else to do what I could do myself. Jesus has never failed me and I never want to feel as though I have failed Him. I believe we are each given a gift.

It has never been a concern or a case of intimidation when the occasion would arise to pray in front of others or to take the hand of someone and pray for a need. I also believe I am called to "stand in the wake" for those who cannot. "Stand in the wake;" to represent, to speak for or on behalf of someone. So I pray; I pray for healing; a new job; a lost soul to turn to Him; I pray for a miracle. I pray for those who cannot or simply choose not to personally seek His solace; for those who need Him, but cannot or choose not to ask.

"Therefore I endure everything for the sake of the elect,
that they too may obtain the salvation
that is in Christ Jesus, with eternal glory."
II Timothy 2:10 (NIV-R)

DATE _____ PRAYER NEED _____
_____

DATE _____ PRAYER NEED _____
_____

DATE _____ PRAYER NEED _____
_____

DATE _____ PRAYER NEED _____
_____

DATE _____ PRAYER NEED _____
_____

DATE _____ PRAYER NEED _____
_____

DATE _____ PRAYER NEED _____
_____

DATE _____ PRAYER NEED _____
_____

DATE _____ PRAYER NEED _____
_____

DATE _____ PRAYER NEED _____
_____

DATE _____PRAYER NEED_____

_____

_____

DATE _____PRAYER NEED_____

_____

_____

DATE _____PRAYER NEED_____

_____

_____

DATE _____PRAYER NEED_____

_____

_____

DATE _____PRAYER NEED_____

_____

_____

DATE _____PRAYER NEED_____

_____

_____

DATE _____PRAYER NEED_____

_____

_____

DATE _____PRAYER NEED_____

_____

_____

Those who know Your name will trust in You, for You, Lord,
have never forsaken those who seek You."
Psalms 9:10 (NIV ®)

Date _____ Prayer Need_____

_____

_____

Date _____ Prayer Need_____

_____

_____

Date _____ Prayer Need_____

_____

_____

Date _____ Prayer Need_____

_____

_____

Notes

_____

_____

_____

_____

_____

_____

_____

_____

_____

_____

_____

_____

ATTITUDE IS EVERYTHING

I hide away in my quiet place, I speak to Him in my quiet voice, I pause and await His response, but I cannot hear Him. Then ... I remember; I begin to really listen by doing what I taught my children. It is not just making a decision to stop what I am doing to fulfill an obligation or a promise to someone. It is the "attitude of prayer," not the constant bidding for His reply that brings us closer to Him and opens our ears to hear His voice.

Attitude; manner, disposition, and feeling should all be considered when we approach Him in prayer. It is the place I choose to be within my heart that creates the perfect attitude I reveal to Him. It is at that exact moment that I truly give Him my attention. I block every other sound, close my eyes and reach out for His touch; feeling the Holy Spirit take over at that moment. There ... He is there ... waiting for us to open our heart and soul to Him; waiting for us to reveal ourselves without hesitation.

"Before they call I will answer;
while they are still speaking, I will hear"
Isaiah 65:24 (NIV R)

DATE _____ PRAYER NEED _____

_____

DATE _____ PRAYER NEED _____

_____

DATE _____ PRAYER NEED _____

_____

DATE _____ PRAYER NEED _____

_____

DATE _____ PRAYER NEED _____

_____

DATE _____ PRAYER NEED _____

_____

DATE _____ PRAYER NEED _____

_____

DATE _____ PRAYER NEED _____

_____

DATE _____ PRAYER NEED _____

_____

DATE _____ PRAYER NEED _____

_____

DATE _____ PRAYER NEED _____

_____

DATE _____ PRAYER NEED _____

_____

DATE _____ PRAYER NEED _____

_____

DATE _____ PRAYER NEED _____

_____

DATE _____ PRAYER NEED _____

_____

DATE _____ PRAYER NEED _____

_____

DATE _____ PRAYER NEED _____

_____

DATE _____ PRAYER NEED _____

_____

*"Call to Me and I will answer you and tell you great
and unsearchable things you do not know"*
Jeremiah 33:3 (NIV ®)

DATE _____ PRAYER NEED_____

_____

DATE _____ PRAYER NEED_____

_____

DATE _____ PRAYER NEED_____

_____

DATE _____ PRAYER NEED_____

_____

NOTES

_____

_____

_____

_____

_____

_____

_____

_____

_____

_____

_____

CLICHÉ, BUT TRUE

On September 27, 2010, I received news that would challenge my faith and change my life. I had been "down-sized" by my company after an eighteen year career. It was a blow to my self-confidence, as well as my faith, but both my girls reminded me that He is simply continuing His plan for my life and with it He lays down a new path ... so I now look at this as an adventure. I am remembering the old cliché, "When God closes a door He opens a window." It is a smaller space and a greater struggle to crawl through, but, never-the-less, it is a start.

My husband and I embrace this time as we learn to rely on His word and His promises, while we grow in our faith and daily exercise our constant trust. I am excited to live out this new chapter of my "walk" with Him, allowing His Holy Spirit to dwell with us and bless my new, chosen profession as a writer. I must add—this also further solidifies the convictions we passed on to our daughters. Once again, they were there for me with words of encouragement and faith in my abilities to make lemonade from the proverbial lemon! I could not love them more!

"Look at the birds of the air;
they do not sow or reap or stow away in barns,
and yet, your heavenly Father feeds them.
Are you not much more valuable than they?"
Matthew 6:26 (NIV®)

DATE _____ PRAYER NEED _____
_____

DATE _____ PRAYER NEED _____
_____

DATE _____ PRAYER NEED _____
_____

DATE _____ PRAYER NEED _____
_____

DATE _____ PRAYER NEED _____
_____

DATE _____ PRAYER NEED _____
_____

DATE _____ PRAYER NEED _____
_____

DATE _____ PRAYER NEED _____
_____

DATE _____ PRAYER NEED _____
_____

DATE _____ PRAYER NEED _____
_____

DATE _____ PRAYER NEED _____

_____

_____

DATE _____ PRAYER NEED _____

_____

_____

DATE _____ PRAYER NEED _____

_____

_____

DATE _____ PRAYER NEED _____

_____

_____

DATE _____ PRAYER NEED _____

_____

_____

DATE _____ PRAYER NEED _____

_____

_____

DATE _____ PRAYER NEED _____

_____

_____

DATE _____ PRAYER NEED _____

_____

_____

"Therefore, do not worry about tomorrow,
for tomorrow will worry about itself.
Each day has enough trouble of its own."
Matthew 6:34 (NIV®)

Date _____ Prayer Need_____
_____
_____

Date _____ Prayer Need_____
_____
_____

Date _____ Prayer Need_____
_____
_____

Date _____ Prayer Need_____
_____
_____

NOTES

_____
_____
_____
_____
_____
_____
_____
_____
_____
_____
_____

EASY TO FORGIVE

Payton, one of our three year-old twin granddaughters, unknowingly, taught us all a lesson on the importance of forgiveness and the selfless expression of love for one another. Her twin sister, Paylon, became upset, faced her sister, and hit Payton directly in the face with the inanimate object she was holding. Without a single hesitation, Payton burst into a flood of tears, as did Paylon, who now realized she was in serious trouble with mom. However, despite the hurtful act, as Payton watched her sister's fears begin to surface, she reached out to her and began to console her, rubbing her back. Through her own pain, bumps, and tears, she spoke with loving tenderness, "No kying sitsy. No kying." Finally, they held each other in a loving embrace. Imagine, knocked to her knees and yet … forgiveness. Without hesitation, she showed compassion and love towards her aggressor. It is humbling when we learn lessons from our children.

I have always looked at forgiveness as a prerequisite to prayer. I prepare myself by asking His forgiveness for my own indiscretions. I clear my mind of any unforgiving thoughts I may hold toward another, so that when I stand to my feet, I can honestly say, "I am so glad I came to you today."

"Bear with each other and forgive whatever grievances
you may have against one another.
Forgive as the Lord forgave you."
Colossians 3:13 (NIV®)

Date _____ Prayer Need _____

_____

_____

Date _____ Prayer Need _____

_____

_____

Date _____ Prayer Need _____

_____

_____

Date _____ Prayer Need _____

_____

_____

Date _____ Prayer Need _____

_____

_____

Date _____ Prayer Need _____

_____

_____

Date _____ Prayer Need _____

_____

_____

Date _____ Prayer Need _____

_____

_____

Date _____ Prayer Need _____

_____

_____

Date _____ Prayer Need _____

_____

_____

DATE _____ PRAYER NEED_____

_____

DATE _____ PRAYER NEED_____

_____

DATE _____ PRAYER NEED_____

_____

DATE _____ PRAYER NEED_____

_____

DATE _____ PRAYER NEED_____

_____

DATE _____ PRAYER NEED_____

_____

DATE _____ PRAYER NEED_____

_____

DATE _____ PRAYER NEED_____

_____

_____

"As far as the east is from the west,
so far has He removed our transgressions from us."
Psalm 103:12 (NIV®)

DATE _____ PRAYER NEED_____

_____

DATE _____ PRAYER NEED_____

_____

DATE _____ PRAYER NEED_____

_____

DATE _____ PRAYER NEED_____

_____

NOTES

_____

_____

_____

_____

_____

_____

_____

_____

_____

_____

_____

A Time for Fresh Faith †

Once again, the day has come to say, "I am on my knees for me." Time to take a breath; time to replenish your spiritual strength; time to seek His guidance and to petition the Lord for yourself; time to ask Him for a refreshing of your spirit.

On the reverse of this page, list the areas in your own life where you desire His help; financial, physical, spiritual, or emotional.

Be willing to remove your shoes and lay face down before Him. He adores you and wants your desires to become His.

Open your heart, call out His name …
Allow Him to offer "Fresh Faith."

"Delight yourself in the Lord
and He will give you the desires of your heart.
Commit your way to the Lord; trust in Him and He will do this:
He will make your righteousness shine like the dawn,
the justice of your cause like the noonday sun."
Psalms 37:4-6 (NIV ®)

MY PRAYER, MY NEEDS

_____

_____

_____

_____

_____

_____

_____

_____

_____

_____

_____

_____

_____

_____

_____

_____

_____

_____

"Do not be anxious about anything, but in everything,
by prayer and petition, with thanksgiving,
present your requests to God .
And the peace of God, which transcends all understanding,
will guard your hearts and your minds in Christ Jesus."
Philippians 4:6-7 (NIV®)

KEEPING IT SIMPLE

When our girls were small, we always ended the evening with the children's prayer, "Now I Lay Me Down to Sleep." It was easy to learn, comforting and the perfect way to instill in them the importance of including Jesus in their life. We changed the last two stanzas, however, to "Watch me Lord through day and night; Keep me in your precious sight." A bit less frightening than educating your child about dying in their sleep! When we were blessed with grandchildren, I began to work on my writing again and added the following new lines:

> Bless mommy, daddy, my family and friends;
> Keep them safe, wrapped in angels wings;
> Make them happy and let them see
> Your love is forever, your forgiveness is free;
> Hold me close and fill my dreams;
> With toys and playmates and heavenly things.

Each of them has a framed copy on the wall in their bedroom.

Why is it, as grown-ups, we make things so difficult? Look at the simplicity of this prayer. We fumble around for the right words to say. Just talk to Him. Keep it simple. He longs to hear our voice.

"This is the assurance we have in approaching God:
that if we ask anything according to His will, he hears us."
I John 5:14 (NIV®)

DATE _____ PRAYER NEED_____
_____

DATE _____ PRAYER NEED_____
_____

DATE _____ PRAYER NEED_____
_____

DATE _____ PRAYER NEED_____
_____

DATE _____ PRAYER NEED_____
_____

DATE _____ PRAYER NEED_____
_____

DATE _____ PRAYER NEED_____
_____

DATE _____ PRAYER NEED_____
_____

DATE _____ PRAYER NEED_____
_____

DATE _____ PRAYER NEED_____
_____

DATE _____ PRAYER NEED_____

_____

_____

DATE _____ PRAYER NEED_____

_____

_____

DATE _____ PRAYER NEED_____

_____

_____

DATE _____ PRAYER NEED_____

_____

_____

DATE _____ PRAYER NEED_____

_____

_____

DATE _____ PRAYER NEED_____

_____

_____

DATE _____ PRAYER NEED_____

_____

_____

DATE _____ PRAYER NEED_____

_____

_____

"And if we know that He hears us—whatever we ask,
—we know that we have what we asked of Him.
1 John 5:15 (NIV®)

Date _____ Prayer Need_____

_____

_____

Date _____ Prayer Need_____

_____

_____

Date _____ Prayer Need_____

_____

_____

Date _____ Prayer Need_____

_____

_____

Notes

_____

_____

_____

_____

_____

_____

_____

_____

_____

_____

_____

_____

No Great Expectations

In John's first letter, he tells us about God's reasons for sending His Son. John writes of the enormous need for us to love one another as God loves us. Our Father in Heaven sent His Son to show His love while He walked among us in hopes that we would *recognize it* in Him. He also explains that Jesus was the atoning sacrifice for our sins. John encourages all of us to love one another in the same way, so that God's love might be completed in us.

We offer prayer, not from obligation or duty, but because of God's love we have been so freely given. He asks simply that we love others without the expectation of anything in return. However, many times over, we have seen God's love, simply from our commitment to prayer and completing what he has requested of His servants … to walk among them, as Jesus did, in hopes that they would *recognize it* in us.

"Dear friends, let us love one another,
for love comes from God.
Everyone who loves has been born of God and knows God.
Whoever does not love,
does not know God, because God is love ."
1 John 4:7-8 (NIVR)

Date _____ Prayer Need_____
_____

Date _____ Prayer Need_____
_____

Date _____ Prayer Need_____
_____

Date _____ Prayer Need_____
_____

Date _____ Prayer Need_____
_____

Date _____ Prayer Need_____
_____

Date _____ Prayer Need_____
_____

Date _____ Prayer Need_____
_____

Date _____ Prayer Need_____
_____

Date _____ Prayer Need_____
_____

DATE _____ PRAYER NEED _____

_____

_____

DATE _____ PRAYER NEED _____

_____

_____

DATE _____ PRAYER NEED _____

_____

_____

DATE _____ PRAYER NEED _____

_____

_____

DATE _____ PRAYER NEED _____

_____

_____

DATE _____ PRAYER NEED _____

_____

_____

DATE _____ PRAYER NEED _____

_____

_____

DATE _____ PRAYER NEED _____

_____

_____

"No one has ever seen God; but if we love each other,
God lives in us and His love is made complete in us."
1 John 4:12 (NIV®)

DATE _____ PRAYER NEED _____
_____
_____

DATE _____ PRAYER NEED _____
_____
_____

DATE _____ PRAYER NEED _____
_____
_____

DATE _____ PRAYER NEED _____
_____
_____

NOTES

_____
_____
_____
_____
_____
_____
_____
_____
_____
_____
_____

SAVORING A MEMORY

When we laid our mother to rest in October 2007, it was requested that family or friends share thoughts or stories at mom's "homecoming" service. It wasn't a difficult decision. I had spoken at Dad's service, a few years prior, and wanted to do the same for Mom. I know she was pleased. Her life had been full of love and joy, surrounded by her children, grandchildren, family and many dear friends.

I spoke of her sweet, welcoming smile, her love of quilting and baking; how she always reached out to others; and how she held a special place in her heart for a child. Mom had volunteered at a children's home in her younger years and had been witness to so much sadness and tragedy; she cradled babies who had never felt a mother's touch; rocked toddlers that hungered for affection; and held youngsters who cried constantly from poor care or neglect. Then I shared a lasting memory Mom left embedded in *my* heart. When she welcomed you, she placed her hands on both sides of your face and, holding you close, left a sweet "mom" kiss on your cheek and then she took a moment to breathe in your fragrance; whether it be your favorite cologne or just you. Her embrace would last only a twinkling, but long enough to embed your memory in her heart. I now do the same, encouraging my children, as well, and today I am encouraging you. Breathe in every moment; embrace every touch and remember that family and friends are numbered among God's most precious gifts.

*"Since my youth, O God, You have taught me, and to this day
I declare your marvelous deeds."*
Psalm 71:17 (NIV®)

Date _____ Prayer Need _____
_____

Date _____ Prayer Need _____
_____

Date _____ Prayer Need _____
_____

Date _____ Prayer Need _____
_____

Date _____ Prayer Need _____
_____

Date _____ Prayer Need _____
_____

Date _____ Prayer Need _____
_____

Date _____ Prayer Need _____
_____

Date _____ Prayer Need _____
_____

Date _____ Prayer Need _____
_____

DATE _____ PRAYER NEED _____

_____

DATE _____ PRAYER NEED _____

_____

DATE _____ PRAYER NEED _____

_____

DATE _____ PRAYER NEED _____

_____

DATE _____ PRAYER NEED _____

_____

DATE _____ PRAYER NEED _____

_____

DATE _____ PRAYER NEED _____

_____

DATE _____ PRAYER NEED _____

_____

_____

"As the Father has loved me, so have I loved you.
Now remain in my love."
John 15:9 (NIV®)

Date _____ Prayer Need _____
_____
_____

Date _____ Prayer Need _____
_____
_____

Date _____ Prayer Need _____
_____
_____

Date _____ Prayer Need _____
_____
_____

NOTES

_____
_____
_____
_____
_____
_____
_____
_____
_____
_____
_____
_____

Believing ... Yet Not Seeing

It always amazes me when I hear individuals question the existence of God. They conjure up ideas and conclusions, permeating the minds of those who are willing to grasp at whatever resolve is available to bring them solace on this earth. Here, where so many choose to worship a *creation* (wealth, possessions, and idols), rather than a *creator.*

I have three year-old twin granddaughters who were born nearly nine weeks premature, a fifteen year-old granddaughter who came home from the hospital and twenty-four hours later, stopped breathing in her mother's arms, a nine year-old grandson who arrived six weeks early and came home with an apparatus to help him breathe. We also have a seven year-old grandson, a twelve year-old granddaughter and a sixteen year-old granddaughter who were all born healthy and strong! I know there are those who would say these living "miracles" were due to skilled doctors or medical intervention, but neither money nor possessions would persuade me to believe that my Heavenly Father did not intervene.

No one will convince me that God does not exist. He is my Creator and my Strength, my Fortress and my Protector, my Counselor and my Joy. He gives me life and gave me all of the above reasons to believe there is a God ... and He is my God!

"Then Jesus told him,
'Because you have seen Me, you have believed;
blessed are those who have not seen and yet have believed.'"
John 20:29 (NIV®)

DATE _____ PRAYER NEED _____
_____

DATE _____ PRAYER NEED _____
_____

DATE _____ PRAYER NEED _____
_____

DATE _____ PRAYER NEED _____
_____

DATE _____ PRAYER NEED _____
_____

DATE _____ PRAYER NEED _____
_____

DATE _____ PRAYER NEED _____
_____

DATE _____ PRAYER NEED _____
_____

DATE _____ PRAYER NEED _____
_____

DATE _____ PRAYER NEED _____
_____

DATE _____ PRAYER NEED _____
_____

DATE _____ PRAYER NEED _____
_____

DATE _____ PRAYER NEED _____
_____

DATE _____ PRAYER NEED _____
_____

DATE _____ PRAYER NEED _____
_____

DATE _____ PRAYER NEED _____
_____

DATE _____ PRAYER NEED _____
_____

DATE _____ PRAYER NEED _____
_____

""For since the creation of the world, God's invisible qualities——
His eternal power and divine nature—— have been clearly seen,
being understood from what has been made,
so that men are without excuse."
Romans 1:20 (NIV®)

Date _____ Prayer Need _____
_____

Date _____ Prayer Need _____
_____

Date _____ Prayer Need _____
_____

Date _____ Prayer Need _____
_____

NOTES

_____
_____
_____
_____
_____
_____
_____
_____
_____
_____
_____

A Time for Fresh Faith ✝

Once again, the day has come to say, "I am on my knees for me." Time to take a breath; time to replenish your spiritual strength; time to seek His guidance and to petition the Lord for yourself; time to ask Him for a refreshing of your spirit.

On the reverse of this page, list the areas in your own life where you desire His help; financial, physical, spiritual, or emotional.

Be willing to remove your shoes and lay face down before Him. He adores you and wants your desires to become His.

Open your heart, call out His name …
Allow Him to offer "Fresh Faith."

"Delight yourself in the Lord
and He will give you the desires of your heart.
Commit your way to the Lord; trust in Him and He will do this:
He will make your righteousness shine like the dawn,
the justice of your cause like the noonday sun."
Psalms 37:4-6 (NIV®)

MY PRAYER, MY NEEDS_____

_____

_____

_____

_____

_____

_____

_____

_____

_____

_____

_____

_____

_____

_____

_____

"Do not be anxious about anything, but in everything,
by prayer and petition, with thanksgiving,
present your requests to God .
And the peace of God, which transcends all understanding,
will guard your hearts and your minds in Christ Jesus."
Philippians 4:6-7 (NIV®)

Perfectly Perfect

Jesus IS our hope, our strength and our only true answer to relief from any pain or fear that we experience. Our request may be to ask that someone "just pray", but not to interpret "just" as though it held little importance, but to say it as to put everything out of our minds, speaking to Him. Go to that place where we think of "just" the Father, our needs and nothing else. Where we can converse with "just" Him, sing praises of His goodness, and thank Him privately for His gifts.

The Thesaurus names many other adjectives that give such specific meaning to the word "just;" simply, really, truly, definitely, emphatically, entirely, completely, and *perfectly*. Perfectly, my favorite … isn't that how we should see Jesus? Perfectly willing to listen; wipe away our tears; hold our hand; offer comfort. He is the only truly perfect presence in our lives. So, "just" pray. Pray for all the needs, all the hurt, all the desires; because He is perfectly able to answer.

"Do not conform any longer to the pattern of this world,
but be transformed by the renewing of your mind.
Then you will be able to test
and approve what God's will is—
His good, pleasing and PERFECT will."
Romans 12:2 (NIV ®)

DATE _____ PRAYER NEED _____

_____

DATE _____ PRAYER NEED _____

_____

DATE _____ PRAYER NEED _____

_____

DATE _____ PRAYER NEED _____

_____

DATE _____ PRAYER NEED _____

_____

DATE _____ PRAYER NEED _____

_____

DATE _____ PRAYER NEED _____

_____

DATE _____ PRAYER NEED _____

_____

DATE _____ PRAYER NEED _____

_____

DATE _____ PRAYER NEED _____

_____

DATE _____ PRAYER NEED _____

_____

_____

DATE _____ PRAYER NEED _____

_____

_____

DATE _____ PRAYER NEED _____

_____

_____

DATE _____ PRAYER NEED _____

_____

_____

DATE _____ PRAYER NEED _____

_____

_____

DATE _____ PRAYER NEED _____

_____

_____

DATE _____ PRAYER NEED _____

_____

_____

DATE _____ PRAYER NEED _____

_____

_____

"God is our refuge and strength, an ever present help in trouble.
Therefore, we will not fear, though the earth give way
and the mountains fall into the heart of the sea ...
(10) 'Be still and know that I am God.'"
Psalms 46:1-2, 10 (NIV®)

105

Date _____ Prayer Need _____
_____
_____

Date _____ Prayer Need _____
_____
_____

Date _____ Prayer Need _____
_____
_____

Date _____ Prayer Need _____
_____
_____

NOTES

_____
_____
_____
_____
_____
_____
_____
_____
_____
_____
_____
_____

THE EYE OF THE BEHOLDER

The word "miracle" is defined by man as "an effect or extraordinary event in the physical world that surpasses all known human or natural powers and is ascribed to a supernatural cause; such an effect or event manifesting or considered as a work of God; a wonder or a marvel." That is certainly an understatement!

The Lord has shown us that continued faith and petitioning can bring about extraordinary events that cause us to believe in miracles where miracles seem completely absent of existence. It is a bit like the rhetorical question, "Is the glass half empty or half full?" Actually, it's both. God's gifts are not always presented in beautiful glittered paper adorned with silver and gold trimmed ribbon; they may appear in a common brown wrapper, loosely tied with twine, but they are still His gifts. It is how we resolve to accept these gifts and the way in which we choose to utilize them that defines them; further defining us and our walk as believers. Open your heart and thank Him for the many gifts in your life. Begin with His gift of forgiveness.

"There are different kinds of gifts,
but the same Spirit.
There are different kinds of service,
but the same Lord."
1 Corinthians 12:4-5 (NIV ®)

DATE _____ PRAYER NEED_____

_____

DATE _____ PRAYER NEED_____

_____

DATE _____ PRAYER NEED_____

_____

DATE _____ PRAYER NEED_____

_____

DATE _____ PRAYER NEED_____

_____

DATE _____ PRAYER NEED_____

_____

DATE _____ PRAYER NEED_____

_____

DATE _____ PRAYER NEED_____

_____

DATE _____ PRAYER NEED_____

_____

DATE _____ PRAYER NEED_____

_____

DATE _____ PRAYER NEED _____

_____

_____

DATE _____ PRAYER NEED _____

_____

DATE _____ PRAYER NEED _____

_____

DATE _____ PRAYER NEED _____

_____

DATE _____ PRAYER NEED _____

_____

DATE _____ PRAYER NEED _____

_____

DATE _____ PRAYER NEED _____

_____

DATE _____ PRAYER NEED _____

_____

_____

"Devote yourselves to prayer,
being watchful and thankful."
Colossians 4:2 (NIV®)

Date _____ Prayer Need _____

Date _____ Prayer Need _____

Date _____ Prayer Need _____

Date _____ Prayer Need _____

NOTES

TRULY FORGIVEN

We carry our mistakes as a burden from past choices. Words spoken in haste, ill-structured decisions, even something as innocent as idle gossip can cause lifelong pain to those who were the unknown recipients of thoughtless spoken words, but our lives are also afflicted. Although we are forgiven by Christ, the difficulty is that we are often unable to forgive ourselves.

It has been said that every sin we commit, every harsh word or wrong act replicates the nails that held our Lord to the cross. We selfishly supplied the nails that were crudely driven through His hands. Those nails represented our transgressions, yet He reached a bleeding, broken hand to each of us in forgiveness. He endured agony and death to set us free. He has forgiven our sins, wiping away those things we regret when we dropped to our knees and asked Him to be our personal Savior. He continues to do so each day in a profound act of selflessness; an act of true forgiveness.

"I, even I, am He who blots out your transgressions,
for My own sake, and remembers your sins no more"
Isaiah 43:25 (NIV®)

DATE _____ PRAYER NEED _____
_____

DATE _____ PRAYER NEED _____
_____

DATE _____ PRAYER NEED _____
_____

DATE _____ PRAYER NEED _____
_____

DATE _____ PRAYER NEED _____
_____

DATE _____ PRAYER NEED _____
_____

DATE _____ PRAYER NEED _____
_____

DATE _____ PRAYER NEED _____
_____

DATE _____ PRAYER NEED _____
_____

DATE _____ PRAYER NEED _____
_____

DATE _____ PRAYER NEED _____

_____

DATE _____ PRAYER NEED _____

_____

DATE _____ PRAYER NEED _____

_____

DATE _____ PRAYER NEED _____

_____

DATE _____ PRAYER NEED _____

_____

DATE _____ PRAYER NEED _____

_____

DATE _____ PRAYER NEED _____

_____

DATE _____ PRAYER NEED _____

_____

"Blessed is he whose transgressions are forgiven,
whose sins are covered.
Blessed is the man whose sin the Lord does not count against him
and in whose spirit is no deceit."
Psalms 32:1-2 (NIV®)

Date _____ Prayer Need _____

_____

Date _____ Prayer Need _____

_____

Date _____ Prayer Need _____

_____

Date _____ Prayer Need _____

_____

Notes

_____
_____
_____
_____
_____
_____
_____
_____
_____
_____
_____

Living the Four C's

Have you ever thought of your life without Christ? Many profess to live a godly life. They testify to being a good person; they don't lie, they don't cheat, they don't steal. They love their family; have a nice home and a great job. It's all good! Yet, living without the promises of Christ brings to mind words spoken during a Sunday morning sermon, many years ago. A life without Christ is a life of four guaranteed truths. Without Him we will be "Condemned" by the law; "Controlled" by the flesh; "Captivated" by the world; and "Conquered" by death.

Regardless of our earthly circumstances, we will not have God's promise of eternal life, only the promises the world allegedly offers us. I want the promise of knowing I am able to depend on the Father, not the world. He offers a written guarantee in His word. I am fully aware that even by knowing Him, my life will never be perfect, void of tragedy, or without painful decisions, but He offers grace and strength to endure these things. He is my constant companion, counselor and teacher. His word helps me to make decisions that will please Him … not the world. Decisions I can live with.

"We have not received the spirit of the world,
but the Spirit who is from God,
that we may understand what God has freely given us."
1 Corinthians 2:12 (NIV®)

DATE _____ PRAYER NEED _____

_____

DATE _____ PRAYER NEED _____

_____

DATE _____ PRAYER NEED _____

_____

DATE _____ PRAYER NEED _____

_____

DATE _____ PRAYER NEED _____

_____

DATE _____ PRAYER NEED _____

_____

DATE _____ PRAYER NEED _____

_____

DATE _____ PRAYER NEED _____

_____

DATE _____ PRAYER NEED _____

_____

DATE _____ PRAYER NEED _____

_____

DATE _____ PRAYER NEED_____

_____

_____

DATE _____ PRAYER NEED_____

_____

_____

DATE _____ PRAYER NEED_____

_____

_____

DATE _____ PRAYER NEED_____

_____

_____

DATE _____ PRAYER NEED_____

_____

_____

DATE _____ PRAYER NEED_____

_____

_____

DATE _____ PRAYER NEED_____

_____

_____

DATE _____ PRAYER NEED_____

_____

_____

"Jesus answered, 'I am the Way, the Truth and the Life.
No one comes to the Father except through Me.'"
John 14:6 (NIV®)

Date _____ Prayer Need _____
_____
_____

Date _____ Prayer Need _____
_____
_____

Date _____ Prayer Need _____
_____
_____

Date _____ Prayer Need _____
_____
_____

Notes

_____
_____
_____
_____
_____
_____
_____
_____
_____
_____
_____
_____

A Time for Fresh Faith ✝

Once again, the day has come to say, "I am on my knees for me." Time to take a breath; time to replenish your spiritual strength; time to seek His guidance and to petition the Lord for yourself; time to ask Him for a refreshing of your spirit.

On the reverse of this page, list the areas in your own life where you desire His help; financial, physical, spiritual, or emotional.

Be willing to remove your shoes and lay face down before Him. He adores you and wants your desires to become His.

Open your heart, call out His name …
Allow Him to offer "Fresh Faith."

"Delight yourself in the Lord
and He will give you the desires of your heart.
Commit your way to the Lord; trust in Him and He will do this:
He will make your righteousness shine like the dawn,
the justice of your cause like the noonday sun."
Psalms 37:4-6 (NIV ®)

MY PRAYER, MY NEEDS

"Do not be anxious about anything, but in everything,
by prayer and petition, with thanksgiving,
present your requests to God.
And the peace of God, which transcends all understanding,
will guard your hearts and your minds in Christ Jesus."
Philippians 4:6-7 (NIV®)

A Breath of Promise

The Lord has been prompting me to share a life changing event that I personally endured in January 1982 when I became extremely ill on a family vacation. Our daughters were two and five and we had been married for eleven years. I was experiencing similar symptoms from the previous month, thought to be the flu, but things turned very serious, very quickly.

With 700 miles ahead of us, we checked into a motel. By six o'clock the following morning, my husband was rushing me to a near-by medical center, stopping on the roadway to administer CPR. Three times that day my heart stopped beating and three times Jesus breathed life back into a lifeless body. I had contracted TSS, Toxic Shock Syndrome, a rare and life threatening illness. I lost nearly all kidney function and was connected to seven separate life supports.

Doctors called it a "Medical Miracle." We knew it was a "Divine Miracle." I was released from the hospital after only seven days and in less than two months, I had nearly full use of both kidneys. But I was not the only recipient of His healing touch, His grace and His mercy during those seven days. Nearly forty beloved saints from our church offered prayer for healing in the hallways of the ICU. Not only for me, but for anyone who would ask. During that time, loved ones were prayed for, hearts were opened and Christ's love was shared.
(Visit www.toxicshock.com)

"I praise you because I am fearfully and wonderfully made;
Your works are wonderful, I know that full well."
Psalms 139:14 (NIV®)

DATE _____ PRAYER NEED _____

_____

DATE _____ PRAYER NEED _____

_____

DATE _____ PRAYER NEED _____

_____

DATE _____ PRAYER NEED _____

_____

DATE _____ PRAYER NEED _____

_____

DATE _____ PRAYER NEED _____

_____

DATE _____ PRAYER NEED _____

_____

DATE _____ PRAYER NEED _____

_____

DATE _____ PRAYER NEED _____

_____

DATE _____ PRAYER NEED _____

_____

DATE _____ PRAYER NEED _____

_____

_____

DATE _____ PRAYER NEED _____

_____

_____

DATE _____ PRAYER NEED _____

_____

_____

DATE _____ PRAYER NEED _____

_____

_____

DATE _____ PRAYER NEED _____

_____

_____

DATE _____ PRAYER NEED _____

_____

_____

DATE _____ PRAYER NEED _____

_____

_____

DATE _____ PRAYER NEED _____

_____

_____

*"I can do everything
through Him who gives me strength."*
Philippians 4:13 (NIV®)

DATE _____ PRAYER NEED _____
_____
_____

DATE _____ PRAYER NEED _____
_____
_____

DATE _____ PRAYER NEED _____
_____
_____

DATE _____ PRAYER NEED _____
_____
_____

NOTES

_____
_____
_____
_____
_____
_____
_____
_____
_____
_____
_____

EASY TO PLEASE

I have been giving serious thought to the accomplishments in my life and, of course, believing that I am lacking some small fulfillment of sorts, I simply could not clear my mind of it … until recently. What have I offered my God, really, other than my life and my faithfulness? Have I made any spectacular discovery, invented something extraordinary, or conceived a long sought cure?

Pondering the subject for some time, I have concluded that what I have accomplished is far more valuable than what I imagined to be of most importance. I have two beautiful daughters. Both love the Lord with all their heart and have lived their lives loving Him and sharing His love to others. I have seven beautiful grandchildren, all destined to know and love Him. I have been married to my high school sweetheart and soul mate for more than forty-one years. We attend a wonderful fellowship, share devotions, spend time in prayer and share His love and grace without hesitation. Although, I have not topped any charts by worldly standards, I believe I have pleased the Lord by living my life in His image and doing so has brought me pleasure, as well. My heart is full, as is my life. I find it does not take giant leaps, just baby steps to honor Him.

"However, I consider my life worth nothing to me,
if only I may finish the race
and complete the task the Lord Jesus has given me——
the task of testifying to the Gospel of God's grace."
Acts 20:24 (NIV®)

DATE _____ PRAYER NEED _____

_____

DATE _____ PRAYER NEED _____

_____

DATE _____ PRAYER NEED _____

_____

DATE _____ PRAYER NEED _____

_____

DATE _____ PRAYER NEED _____

_____

DATE _____ PRAYER NEED _____

_____

DATE _____ PRAYER NEED _____

_____

DATE _____ PRAYER NEED _____

_____

DATE _____ PRAYER NEED _____

_____

DATE _____ PRAYER NEED _____

_____

DATE _____ PRAYER NEED _____

_____

DATE _____ PRAYER NEED _____

_____

DATE _____ PRAYER NEED _____

_____

DATE _____ PRAYER NEED _____

_____

DATE _____ PRAYER NEED _____

_____

DATE _____ PRAYER NEED _____

_____

DATE _____ PRAYER NEED _____

_____

DATE _____ PRAYER NEED _____

_____

_____

*"And whatever you do, whether in word or deed,
do it all in the name of the Lord Jesus,
giving thanks to God the Father through Him."*
Colossians 3:17 (NIV®)

Date _____ Prayer Need _____

_____

Date _____ Prayer Need _____

_____

Date _____ Prayer Need _____

_____

Date _____ Prayer Need _____

_____

NOTES

_____

_____

_____

_____

_____

_____

_____

_____

_____

_____

MERCY BEYOND MEASURE

Mercy is described as an act of kindness, compassion, pity, or benevolence; the discretionary power of a judge to pardon an offender. Mercy shows evidence of divine favor. I cannot speak for anyone else, but, in my life, my God has been merciful beyond measure. I have no reason to believe that I am worthy of His mercy, His grace, or His love. We are not asked by God to earn our way in order to receive these gifts. He freely gives them to us when we surrender our lives to Him. God sent His Son to die for our sins, without hesitation and without regret. I can only imagine the sadness on the holy face of God, when His sinless Son knelt in the garden, asking that this cup of suffering, separation from His Father, and ultimate death be taken from Him, knowing full well the answer; all in exchange for the pardon of our sins.

We continue to serve a loving God and, although, he allows us to make irresponsible choices, perform foolish acts and sometimes speak painful words, we need only ask and He will continue to forgive and offer us kindness, compassion, and the gift of mercy.

"He who conceals his sins does not prosper,
but whoever confesses and renounces them finds mercy."
Proverbs 28:13 (NIV®)

DATE _____ PRAYER NEED _____
_____

DATE _____ PRAYER NEED _____
_____

DATE _____ PRAYER NEED _____
_____

DATE _____ PRAYER NEED _____
_____

DATE _____ PRAYER NEED _____
_____

DATE _____ PRAYER NEED _____
_____

DATE _____ PRAYER NEED _____
_____

DATE _____ PRAYER NEED _____
_____

DATE _____ PRAYER NEED _____
_____

DATE _____ PRAYER NEED _____
_____

DATE _____ PRAYER NEED _____

_____

_____

DATE _____ PRAYER NEED _____

_____

_____

DATE _____ PRAYER NEED _____

_____

_____

DATE _____ PRAYER NEED _____

_____

_____

DATE _____ PRAYER NEED _____

_____

_____

DATE _____ PRAYER NEED _____

_____

_____

DATE _____ PRAYER NEED _____

_____

_____

DATE _____ PRAYER NEED _____

_____

_____

"But you, O' Lord, are a compassionate and gracious God,
slow to anger, abounding in love and faithfulness."
Psalms 86:15 (NIV®)

Date _____ Prayer Need _____

_____

Date _____ Prayer Need _____

_____

Date _____ Prayer Need _____

_____

Date _____ Prayer Need _____

_____

NOTES

_____

_____

_____

_____

_____

_____

_____

_____

_____

_____

FOREVER AND EVER

Our earthly relationships endure a measure of emotions from joy, happiness and passion to fear, anger and pain, but the one relationship that extends beyond worldly explanation is the personal relationship we can choose to have with Christ; a relationship that gives us hope, joy, peace and fulfillment. Sin separated us from Him, but we have the choice to form a perfect bond, a bond that has no worldly definition or understanding, except to others who have made the same perfect choice. Once bound to Him, there should be no separation.

Each day, speak to Him; asking what He wants of you. What will you lay at His feet today? It is at His feet; touching the hem of His robe that builds that "eternal" bond. That's where you are when you place your heart in His hands. Lay your past, present and future at His feet … past regrets, past mistakes, future decisions and dreams. Nothing … absolutely nothing compares.

"Now that you have purified yourselves by obeying the truth
so that you have sincere love for your brothers,
love one another deeply, from the heart."
1 Peter 1:22 (NIV R)

Date _____ Prayer Need_____

_____

Date _____ Prayer Need_____

_____

Date _____ Prayer Need_____

_____

Date _____ Prayer Need_____

_____

Date _____ Prayer Need_____

_____

Date _____ Prayer Need_____

_____

Date _____ Prayer Need_____

_____

Date _____ Prayer Need_____

_____

Date _____ Prayer Need_____

_____

Date _____ Prayer Need_____

_____

DATE _____ PRAYER NEED _____

_____

_____

DATE _____ PRAYER NEED _____

_____

_____

DATE _____ PRAYER NEED _____

_____

_____

DATE _____ PRAYER NEED _____

_____

_____

DATE _____ PRAYER NEED _____

_____

_____

DATE _____ PRAYER NEED _____

_____

_____

DATE _____ PRAYER NEED _____

_____

_____

DATE _____ PRAYER NEED _____

_____

_____

"Be completely humble and gentle;
be patient, bearing with one another in love.
Make every effort to keep the unity of the Spirit
through the bond of peace."
Ephesians 4:2-3 (NIV®)

DATE _____ PRAYER NEED _____

_____

DATE _____ PRAYER NEED _____

_____

DATE _____ PRAYER NEED _____

_____

DATE _____ PRAYER NEED _____

_____

NOTES

_____

_____

_____

_____

_____

_____

_____

_____

_____

_____

A Time for Fresh Faith ✝

Once again, the day has come to say, "I am on my knees for me." Time to take a breath; time to replenish your spiritual strength; time to seek His guidance and to petition the Lord for yourself; time to ask Him for a refreshing of your spirit.

On the reverse of this page, list the areas in your own life where you desire His help; financial, physical, spiritual, or emotional.

Be willing to remove your shoes and lay face down before Him. He adores you and wants your desires to become His.

Open your heart, call out His name …
Allow Him to offer "Fresh Faith."

"Delight yourself in the Lord
and He will give you the desires of your heart.
Commit your way to the Lord; trust in Him and He will do this:
He will make your righteousness shine like the dawn,
the justice of your cause like the noonday sun."
Psalms 37:4-6 (NIV®)

MY PRAYER, MY NEEDS

_____

_____

_____

_____

_____

_____

_____

_____

_____

_____

_____

_____

_____

_____

_____

_____

_____

_____

_____

"Do not be anxious about anything, but in everything,
by prayer and petition, with thanksgiving,
present your requests to God .
And the peace of God, which transcends all understanding,
will guard your hearts and your minds in Christ Jesus."
Philippians 4:6-7 (NIV®)

SPIRITUAL RENEWAL

The "New Millennium," words that conjured up marvelous images of second chances, new found prosperity, a promise of a revived America. Did you know that "Millennium" is defined as, "A time of peace and happiness, especially in the distant future?" Perhaps, for some, it was easy to forget our present source of peace and happiness. I know I was guilty of the same. When the calendar turned to the year 2000 my husband required his second back surgery in February; I was diagnosed with skin cancer in May; Dad passed in July; because of his surgery, my husband found himself unemployed in August; and was later diagnosed with a pre-cancer in September. It was anything but a prosperous "New Millennium". But there was something new … a stirring within us that clearly revealed a new found desire to serve the Lord with all our hearts. It was a renewal of our spirit, our strengths, and our commitment to each other; a renewed understanding of our "distant future" with Him.

In retrospect, yes, it was disappointing to have experienced so much pain, heartache and worry, but we made it through a tough year. God never said life in this earthly place we call home would be easy, but He did promise to be there with us should we need to reach up for His hand and be pulled from the wreckage. Wreckage, more often than not, we have created ourselves.

"There is a time for everything,
and a season for every activity under heaven..."
Ecclesiastes 3:1 (NIV R)

DATE _____ PRAYER NEED _____

_____

DATE _____ PRAYER NEED _____

_____

DATE _____ PRAYER NEED _____

_____

DATE _____ PRAYER NEED _____

_____

DATE _____ PRAYER NEED _____

_____

DATE _____ PRAYER NEED _____

_____

DATE _____ PRAYER NEED _____

_____

DATE _____ PRAYER NEED _____

_____

DATE _____ PRAYER NEED _____

_____

DATE _____ PRAYER NEED _____

_____

DATE _____ PRAYER NEED _____

DATE _____ PRAYER NEED _____

DATE _____ PRAYER NEED _____

DATE _____ PRAYER NEED _____

DATE _____ PRAYER NEED _____

DATE _____ PRAYER NEED _____

DATE _____ PRAYER NEED _____

DATE _____ PRAYER NEED _____

"O Lord, our Lord, how majestic is your name in all the earth!
You have set your glory above the heavens."
Psalm 8:1 (NIV®)

DATE _____ PRAYER NEED _____
_____

DATE _____ PRAYER NEED _____
_____

DATE _____ PRAYER NEED _____
_____

DATE _____ PRAYER NEED _____
_____

NOTES

_____
_____
_____
_____
_____
_____
_____
_____
_____
_____
_____
_____

BRING IT HOME

Fellowship is a cherished gift from one believer to another. We find fellowship in the body of believers in our church and cherish every moment, shaking hands, offering an embrace of comfort, learning from the word and offering prayer. But what happens when we walk from the altar and through the door, back to what is the normalcy in our everyday lives? We desperately attempt to live our church life at home, at work, at school. We need to find that place where we can live our personal life with Jesus included. To know Him is to look beyond the temporary sanctity of our church.

Knowing God is not just within our behavior, it's truly "living" Him. It is calling a friend in the middle of a busy week to offer prayer or a word of encouragement. It is giving praise to our children and our spouse; being a spiritual witness to our extended family, as well as in our community. It is trusting that He will provide provisions to feed, clothe and shelter us. It is loving and trusting the Father away from the security of His house and inviting Him to follow us … beyond the door.

"We proclaim to you what we have seen and heard,
so that you also may have fellowship with us.
And our fellowship is with the Father
and with His Son, Jesus Christ"
1 John 1:3 (NIV ®)

DATE _____ PRAYER NEED _____
_____

DATE _____ PRAYER NEED _____
_____

DATE _____ PRAYER NEED _____
_____

DATE _____ PRAYER NEED _____
_____

DATE _____ PRAYER NEED _____
_____

DATE _____ PRAYER NEED _____
_____

DATE _____ PRAYER NEED _____
_____

DATE _____ PRAYER NEED _____
_____

DATE _____ PRAYER NEED _____
_____

DATE _____ PRAYER NEED _____
_____

DATE _____ PRAYER NEED _____

_____

_____

DATE _____ PRAYER NEED _____

_____

_____

DATE _____ PRAYER NEED _____

_____

_____

DATE _____ PRAYER NEED _____

_____

_____

DATE _____ PRAYER NEED _____

_____

_____

DATE _____ PRAYER NEED _____

_____

_____

DATE _____ PRAYER NEED _____

_____

_____

DATE _____ PRAYER NEED _____

_____

_____

"But if we walk in the light, as He is in the light ,
we have fellowship with one another,
and the blood of Jesus, His Son,
purifies us from every sin."
1 John 1:7 (NIV®)

DATE _____ PRAYER NEED _____

_____

_____

DATE _____ PRAYER NEED _____

_____

_____

DATE _____ PRAYER NEED _____

_____

_____

DATE _____ PRAYER NEED _____

_____

_____

NOTES

_____

_____

_____

_____

_____

_____

_____

_____

_____

_____

_____

_____

NEW FOUND HOPE

We all have our own characterization of "pain". Our pain is personal and cannot be felt by anyone else in the same form or the same intensity. Pain can be expressed as physical, emotional, or spiritual. It may be described as misery, sadness, anguish, or fear; whatever the case, it is ours and ours alone. Still, as Christians, we have a Savior helping us to endure.

I am reminded of a story about a young couple, expecting their first child. They held each other closely, watching as their home burned from a neighbor's carelessly ignored rubbish fire. The flames blended poetically with a radiant sunset as they dropped to their knees praying for some fragment of hope in this devastation. The following day, the couple sifted through the smoldering embers for any remnant of their lives together. They uncovered a pewter frame, unscathed, containing an ultrasound of their unborn son … a blessing, yet to come.

It is difficult, if not seemingly impossible for some, to find hope when we are hurting, but we need to look for the one small shred of evidence that there is good that will come. Whatever the enormity of our sorrow; the loss of a friend or loved one; financial fears; physical losses; past mistakes, we need to search it out and grab ahold. This and only this is what will carry us through the pain. Trust Him. He is there to transform your grief to glory.

"All these blessings will come upon you and accompany you if you obey the Lord your God..."
Deuteronomy 28:2 (NIV R)

DATE _____ PRAYER NEED _____
_____

DATE _____ PRAYER NEED _____
_____

DATE _____ PRAYER NEED _____
_____

DATE _____ PRAYER NEED _____
_____

DATE _____ PRAYER NEED _____
_____

DATE _____ PRAYER NEED _____
_____

DATE _____ PRAYER NEED _____
_____

DATE _____ PRAYER NEED _____
_____

DATE _____ PRAYER NEED _____
_____

DATE _____ PRAYER NEED _____
_____

DATE _____ PRAYER NEED _____

_____

_____

DATE _____ PRAYER NEED _____

_____

DATE _____ PRAYER NEED _____

_____

DATE _____ PRAYER NEED _____

_____

DATE _____ PRAYER NEED _____

_____

DATE _____ PRAYER NEED _____

_____

DATE _____ PRAYER NEED _____

_____

DATE _____ PRAYER NEED _____

_____

_____

"Praise be to the God and Father of our Lord Jesus Christ,
Who has blessed us in the heavenly realms
with every spiritual blessing in Christ."
Ephesians 1:3 (NIV®)

DATE _____ PRAYER NEED _____
_____
_____

DATE _____ PRAYER NEED _____
_____
_____

DATE _____ PRAYER NEED _____
_____
_____

DATE _____ PRAYER NEED _____
_____
_____

NOTES

_____
_____
_____
_____
_____
_____
_____
_____
_____
_____
_____
_____

FORGET SHOES

The bulletin board suspended above my office desk is adorned with several personal and inspirational pieces. There is a picture of me with my sister and brother taken the day we laid mom to rest, a postcard stating "Believe in Your Dreams," a small photo of a mouse wearing a tiny red helmet; assessing the ability to snatch the cheese from a trap without his demise. The quote above his head declares, "Be determined in achieving your goals!" In the center of the board is a large wooden plaque adorned with a bright green, satin ribbon and bordered with pink and white polka dots, proclaiming, "Put on your BIG girl panties and deal with it!" A gift from my youngest daughter, ironically, just a few short months prior to being downsized from my career of eighteen years. But my favorite is a card my husband gave me on my fiftieth birthday.

Knowing my unconventional certitude regarding the need for shoes and finding discarded slippers, tennis shoes and flip-flops in every room, it says, simply ... "Forget Shoes;" displaying only the bottoms of two small feet nestled in grass and the ruffled hem of a pink and white checkered dress. That statement stirred my thoughts ... forget shoes? Hmmm ... forget our worldly interferences, forget our day-to-day issues. Come to the Father stripped to our bare feet; walking on holy ground, dropping to our knees, giving our all to Him ... leaving our "shoes" behind.

"I will give you a new heart and put a new spirit in you;
I will remove from you your heart of stone
and will give you a heart of flesh."
Ezekiel 36:26 (NIV®)

DATE _____ PRAYER NEED _____

_____

DATE _____ PRAYER NEED _____

_____

DATE _____ PRAYER NEED _____

_____

DATE _____ PRAYER NEED _____

_____

DATE _____ PRAYER NEED _____

_____

DATE _____ PRAYER NEED _____

_____

DATE _____ PRAYER NEED _____

_____

DATE _____ PRAYER NEED _____

_____

DATE _____ PRAYER NEED _____

_____

DATE _____ PRAYER NEED _____

_____

DATE _____ PRAYER NEED _____

_____

_____

DATE _____ PRAYER NEED _____

_____

_____

DATE _____ PRAYER NEED _____

_____

_____

DATE _____ PRAYER NEED _____

_____

_____

DATE _____ PRAYER NEED _____

_____

_____

DATE _____ PRAYER NEED _____

_____

_____

DATE _____ PRAYER NEED _____

_____

_____

DATE _____ PRAYER NEED _____

_____

_____

"Nothing in all creation is hidden from God's sight.
Everything is uncovered
and laid bare before the eyes of Him to
Whom we must give account."
Hebrews 4:13 (NIV®)

DATE _____ PRAYER NEED _____

_____

_____

DATE _____ PRAYER NEED _____

_____

_____

DATE _____ PRAYER NEED _____

_____

_____

DATE _____ PRAYER NEED _____

_____

_____

NOTES

_____

_____

_____

_____

_____

_____

_____

_____

_____

_____

_____

_____

A Time for Fresh Faith †

Once again, the day has come to say, "I am on my knees for me." Time to take a breath; time to replenish your spiritual strength; time to seek His guidance and to petition the Lord for yourself; time to ask Him for a refreshing of your spirit.

On the reverse of this page, list the areas in your own life where you desire His help; financial, physical, spiritual, or emotional.

Be willing to remove your shoes and lay face down before Him. He adores you and wants your desires to become His.

Open your heart, call out His name …
Allow Him to offer "Fresh Faith."

"Delight yourself in the Lord
and He will give you the desires of your heart.
Commit your way to the Lord; trust in Him and He will do this:
He will make your righteousness shine like the dawn,
the justice of your cause like the noonday sun."
Psalms 37:4-6 (NIV®)

My Prayer, My Needs

_____

_____

_____

_____

_____

_____

_____

_____

_____

_____

_____

_____

_____

_____

_____

_____

"Do not be anxious about anything, but in everything,
by prayer and petition, with thanksgiving,
present your requests to God .
And the peace of God, which transcends all understanding,
will guard your hearts and your minds in Christ Jesus."
Philippians 4:6-7 (NIV®)

JUST ROUTINE

While sitting at my desk and nearing the end of the day, I glanced over my shoulder to see if our five year-old Labradoodle, Lilly, was still sleeping on the landing at the top of the stairs. She often took naps there, giving her the ability to see both my office and the room to which my husband would often retreat for a little relaxation at the end of his busy day. I have concluded that it must give her a sense of security and firm assurance that we are both nearby. At that very moment, a bright streak of color abruptly struck the adjacent wall. So as not to disturb her napping, I quickly, but quietly, hurried to the landing window and peered out toward the field of wheat behind our home.

The sun was setting, creating a blaze of orange, yellow and red across the horizon, illuminating through the trees, and striking the wall with intensity and beauty. It was, yet again, another reminder of our Lord's amazing greatness. I glanced down at Lilly as she stared up at me, almost to say, "You know, He does that every day." I leaned down and gave her ears a rub. She tipped her head, planted a wet kiss on my wrist, and returned to her nap.

We never choose to take His gifts for granted, but our lives can become so intertwined with schedules and commitments, we neglect to take time to absorb His offer of daily blessings, even something as routine as a sunset.

"... He who appoints the sun to shine by day, Who decrees the moon and stars to shine by night, Who stirs up the sea so that its waves roar——the Lord Almighty is His name."
Jeremiah 31:35 (NIV®)

DATE _____ PRAYER NEED _____

_____

DATE _____ PRAYER NEED _____

_____

DATE _____ PRAYER NEED _____

_____

DATE _____ PRAYER NEED _____

_____

DATE _____ PRAYER NEED _____

_____

DATE _____ PRAYER NEED _____

_____

DATE _____ PRAYER NEED _____

_____

DATE _____ PRAYER NEED _____

_____

DATE _____ PRAYER NEED _____

_____

DATE _____ PRAYER NEED _____

_____

DATE _____ PRAYER NEED _____

_____

DATE _____ PRAYER NEED _____

_____

DATE _____ PRAYER NEED _____

_____

DATE _____ PRAYER NEED _____

_____

DATE _____ PRAYER NEED _____

_____

DATE _____ PRAYER NEED _____

_____

DATE _____ PRAYER NEED _____

_____

DATE _____ PRAYER NEED _____

_____

_____

"In the beginning,
God created the heavens and the earth."
Genesis 1:1 (NIV®)

DATE _____ PRAYER NEED _____

_____

DATE _____ PRAYER NEED _____

_____

DATE _____ PRAYER NEED _____

_____

DATE _____ PRAYER NEED _____

_____

NOTES

_____

_____

_____

_____

_____

_____

_____

_____

_____

_____

_____

FROM BOYS TO MEN

Both our grandsons have reached the ever popular "that's not fair" juncture in their adolescent lives and are exhibiting their feelings more often than usual these days. With all the new toys and electronic gadgets that have hit the market in the 21st century, our children are in jeopardy of becoming more and more consumed by the ploys of the media. Eliminating these "influences" from our home would be a simple solution, but it is difficult to protect them from the flood of temptation at shopping malls, schools or our own neighborhood. The boys will retreat to their rooms to cry, to pout or simply to prove their displeasure with Mom or Dad, but their parents know best and want their boys to make choices that will mold them into the godly men they see in their future.

Keeping our children out of harm's way, teaching them good morals and helping them to make prudent choices and find godly alternatives are tasks entrusted to earthly parents. Showing them grace, mercy and forgiveness is a responsibility our heavenly Father gladly accepts and a gift He lovingly offers to those who will simply ask.

"I have no greater joy than to hear
that my children are walking in the truth"
3 John 1:4 (NIV®)

DATE _____ PRAYER NEED _____
_____

DATE _____ PRAYER NEED _____
_____

DATE _____ PRAYER NEED _____
_____

DATE _____ PRAYER NEED _____
_____

DATE _____ PRAYER NEED _____
_____

DATE _____ PRAYER NEED _____
_____

DATE _____ PRAYER NEED _____
_____

DATE _____ PRAYER NEED _____
_____

DATE _____ PRAYER NEED _____
_____

DATE _____ PRAYER NEED _____
_____

DATE _____ PRAYER NEED _____

_____

_____

DATE _____ PRAYER NEED _____

_____

_____

DATE _____ PRAYER NEED _____

_____

_____

DATE _____ PRAYER NEED _____

_____

_____

DATE _____ PRAYER NEED _____

_____

_____

DATE _____ PRAYER NEED _____

_____

_____

DATE _____ PRAYER NEED _____

_____

_____

DATE _____ PRAYER NEED _____

_____

_____

"Sons are a heritage from the Lord,
children a reward from Him.
Like arrows in the hands of a warrior
are sons born in one's youth"
Psalm 127: 3-4 (NIV/R)

DATE _____ PRAYER NEED _____

_____

DATE _____ PRAYER NEED _____

_____

DATE _____ PRAYER NEED _____

_____

DATE _____ PRAYER NEED _____

_____

_____

NOTES

_____

_____

_____

_____

_____

_____

_____

_____

_____

_____

_____

A MASTER PLAN

On a warm summer evening, we loaded an ice chest, grabbed some blankets and drove our pick-up to the only drive-in theater in a one hundred mile radius; twenty miles into the countryside. As empty nesters, the movie choice is much simpler (eliminating Disney movies … although we still love them and own them all on VHS … for the grandchildren, of course), but, during a moment, void of sanity … we bought a family dog. Lilly is a five year-old Labradoodle. She is passionately devoted to my husband and seems to be always under foot, but we love her and she accompanies us whenever possible. We arrived a bit early, located the perfect viewing spot and settled in to "people" watch.

Our solitude was soon interrupted when the fifty foot screen suddenly illuminated with animated dancing boxes of candy, popcorn, and soda, while the speaker resounded with unrecognizable music at a decibel range beyond human tolerance. My husband fumbled for the volume control, but the chaos was more than Lilly could comprehend. She began to bark incessantly——at the twenty foot dancing candy bar; at the enormous soda cup spilling over onto the cars below. She was terrified! When we were finally able to calm her, she curled up on Robert's lap. She tips the scales at seventy pounds … not a small dog by any means, but she knew exactly where to go for the protection and the comfort she was seeking … she went to her master.

"...but those who hope in the Lord will renew their strength.
They will soar on wings like eagles;
they will run and not grow weary,
they will walk and not faint."
Isaiah 40:31 (NIV®)

Date _____ Prayer Need _____

_____

Date _____ Prayer Need _____

_____

Date _____ Prayer Need _____

_____

Date _____ Prayer Need _____

_____

Date _____ Prayer Need _____

_____

Date _____ Prayer Need _____

_____

Date _____ Prayer Need _____

_____

Date _____ Prayer Need _____

_____

Date _____ Prayer Need _____

_____

Date _____ Prayer Need _____

_____

DATE _____ PRAYER NEED _____

_____

_____

DATE _____ PRAYER NEED _____

_____

_____

DATE _____ PRAYER NEED _____

_____

_____

DATE _____ PRAYER NEED _____

_____

_____

DATE _____ PRAYER NEED _____

_____

_____

DATE _____ PRAYER NEED _____

_____

_____

DATE _____ PRAYER NEED _____

_____

_____

DATE _____ PRAYER NEED _____

_____

_____

"He gives strength to the weary
and increases the power of the weak."
Isaiah 40:29 (NIV®)

Date _____ Prayer Need _____

_____

_____

Date _____ Prayer Need _____

_____

_____

Date _____ Prayer Need _____

_____

_____

Date _____ Prayer Need _____

_____

_____

NOTES

_____

_____

_____

_____

_____

_____

_____

_____

_____

_____

_____

_____

THY WILL BE DONE

As a woman of faith, a wife, and mother, I spend much of my time in prayer. Whether physically on my knees or simply conversing with the Lord throughout my day, prayer is my constant source of communication. I am also aware that when I pray, there is the unspoken rule always to ask that His will be done. Admittedly, it is sometimes a hesitant request. As Christ knelt in the garden asking His heavenly Father to "remove this cup" from Him, He also spoke, "... not my will, but thine, be done." Even Christ knew that He must submit to the will of the Father.

Praying for healing; a life changing decision; a relationship, are all areas where we seek His guidance, but we fear what we are asking for is not His desire. We fear saying the words, "thy will be done" as much as we fear the purpose of our prayer. The passage also states that an angel from heaven appeared to Jesus in the garden and strengthened Him. There is a song that we sing in our fellowship that speaks of the personal relationship Christ has with each of us. It is a reminder, "He knows our every thought; He sees each tear that falls." Trusting Him is the only way to surrender to His will and gain peace, knowing that He is in control and the outcome is as it should be ... within His will.

"Father, if you are willing, take this cup from Me;
yet not My will, but Yours be done.
An angel from heaven appeared to Him
and strengthened Him."
Luke 22:42-43 (NIV R)

DATE _____ PRAYER NEED _____
_____

DATE _____ PRAYER NEED _____
_____

DATE _____ PRAYER NEED _____
_____

DATE _____ PRAYER NEED _____
_____

DATE _____ PRAYER NEED _____
_____

DATE _____ PRAYER NEED _____
_____

DATE _____ PRAYER NEED _____
_____

DATE _____ PRAYER NEED _____
_____

DATE _____ PRAYER NEED _____
_____

DATE _____ PRAYER NEED _____
_____

DATE _____ PRAYER NEED _____
_____

DATE _____ PRAYER NEED _____
_____

DATE _____ PRAYER NEED _____
_____

DATE _____ PRAYER NEED _____
_____

DATE _____ PRAYER NEED _____
_____

DATE _____ PRAYER NEED _____
_____

DATE _____ PRAYER NEED _____
_____

DATE _____ PRAYER NEED _____
_____
_____

"Blessed is he whose help is in the God of Jacob,
whose hope is in the Lord his God,
the Maker of heaven and earth ... "
Psalm 146:5 (NIV ®)

Date _____ Prayer Need_____

_____

Date _____ Prayer Need_____

_____

Date _____ Prayer Need_____

_____

Date _____ Prayer Need_____

_____

NOTES

_____

_____

_____

_____

_____

_____

_____

_____

_____

_____

_____

A Time for Fresh Faith ✝

Once again, the day has come to say, "I am on my knees for me." Time to take a breath; time to replenish your spiritual strength; time to seek His guidance and to petition the Lord for yourself; time to ask Him for a refreshing of your spirit.

On the reverse of this page, list the areas in your own life where you desire His help; financial, physical, spiritual, or emotional.

Be willing to remove your shoes and lay face down before Him. He adores you and wants your desires to become His.

Open your heart, call out His name …
Allow Him to offer "Fresh Faith."

"Delight yourself in the Lord
and He will give you the desires of your heart.
Commit your way to the Lord; trust in Him and He will do this:
He will make your righteousness shine like the dawn,
the justice of your cause like the noonday sun."
Psalms 37:4-6 (NIV R)

MY PRAYER, MY NEEDS

_"Do not be anxious about anything, but in everything,
by prayer and petition, with thanksgiving,
present your requests to God.
And the peace of God, which transcends all understanding,
will guard your hearts and your minds in Christ Jesus."
Philippians 4:6-7_ (NIV®)

Keeping the "Piece"

I have been reflecting on a statement from some years back, "Don't let your past dictate your future." Although, for some, our past can be a place of perfect choices, lasting relationships and fond memories; for others it may also be a compilation of poor choices, broken relationships, and painful memories. Knowing Jesus can change everything. Our lives don't need to be a constant reminder of the past. We now have the opportunity to create a present and a future that will reflect the blessings we have acquired since we took that glorious step to know Christ as our Savior. We cannot waste precious time in this relationship concerning ourselves with yesterday's transgressions.

There are always pieces of our past that have shaped our future, but those are the well-fitted pieces; pieces of the puzzle that were necessary to bring us to where we are today. But the pieces that are unnecessary and painful are the ones we must turn loose. Psalm 103:11-12 reads, "For as high as the heavens are above the earth, so great is His love for those who fear him; as far as the east is from the west, He removed our transgressions from us." No matter how you define your past, trust Christ to define your future.

"For I will forgive their wickedness
and will remember their sins no more."
Hebrews 8:12 (NIV®)

Date _____ Prayer Need _____

_____

_____

Date _____ Prayer Need _____

_____

_____

Date _____ Prayer Need _____

_____

_____

Date _____ Prayer Need _____

_____

_____

Date _____ Prayer Need _____

_____

_____

Date _____ Prayer Need _____

_____

_____

Date _____ Prayer Need _____

_____

_____

Date _____ Prayer Need _____

_____

_____

Date _____ Prayer Need _____

_____

_____

Date _____ Prayer Need _____

_____

_____

DATE _____PRAYER NEED_____

_____

DATE _____PRAYER NEED_____

_____

DATE _____PRAYER NEED_____

_____

DATE _____PRAYER NEED_____

_____

DATE _____PRAYER NEED_____

_____

DATE _____PRAYER NEED_____

_____

DATE _____PRAYER NEED_____

_____

DATE _____PRAYER NEED_____

_____

"Remember not the sins of my youth and my rebellious ways;
according to your love remember me,
for you are good O Lord."
Psalm 24:7 (NIV®)

Date _____ Prayer Need _____

_____

Date _____ Prayer Need _____

_____

Date _____ Prayer Need _____

_____

Date _____ Prayer Need _____

_____

NOTES

_____

_____

_____

_____

_____

_____

_____

_____

_____

_____

_____

OUR YELLOW BRICK ROAD

"The plan" for your life is in place before you take a single breath, even if we are determined to take a turn in the road and go against God's lead.

We relocated our family to Oregon, believing in our hearts, it was His will for us. We were determined to raise our children away from the "big city" influences and give them every opportunity allowable. However, we left our extended family in California, giving us reason to cast doubt as to whether this truly was God's direction. We returned three times over a six-year span, in a vain attempt to re-map "the plan," each time, feeling Him tugging at our hearts to come back to Oregon. We tried to change "the plan" without success. We stopped trying twenty-five years ago and our children are grown and happy in so many ways.

We will all attempt to map our own course; whether we take the "high road," or the "low road," we must first learn to trust Him; allowing Him to lead us; allowing Him to offer His counsel and direction; allowing Him to pave the way. In each life, there is given the opportunity to be within His perfect plan … a plan created, even before we took a single breath.

"In everything that he undertook in the service of God's temple
and in obedience to the law and the commands,
he sought his God and worked wholeheartedly.
And so he prospered."
2 Chronicles 31:21 (NIV®)

DATE _____ PRAYER NEED _____
_____

DATE _____ PRAYER NEED _____
_____

DATE _____ PRAYER NEED _____
_____

DATE _____ PRAYER NEED _____
_____

DATE _____ PRAYER NEED _____
_____

DATE _____ PRAYER NEED _____
_____

DATE _____ PRAYER NEED _____
_____

DATE _____ PRAYER NEED _____
_____

DATE _____ PRAYER NEED _____
_____

DATE _____ PRAYER NEED _____
_____

DATE _____ PRAYER NEED _____
_____

DATE _____ PRAYER NEED _____
_____

DATE _____ PRAYER NEED _____
_____

DATE _____ PRAYER NEED _____
_____

DATE _____ PRAYER NEED _____
_____

DATE _____ PRAYER NEED _____
_____

DATE _____ PRAYER NEED _____
_____

DATE _____ PRAYER NEED _____
_____

"Many are the plans in a man's heart,
but it is the Lord's purpose that prevails."
Proverbs 19:21 (NIV®)

DATE _____ PRAYER NEED _____

_____

DATE _____ PRAYER NEED _____

_____

DATE _____ PRAYER NEED _____

_____

DATE _____ PRAYER NEED _____

_____

NOTES

_____

_____

_____

_____

_____

_____

_____

_____

_____

_____

_____

_____

IT'S WHAT WE DO

"Worrying does not take away tomorrow's troubles … it takes away today's peace." I cannot remember the origin of this quote, but only that I believe it to be a solid truth in my life. Jesus spoke all about the worries of the world in Matthew, chapter six. He tells us that our heavenly Father knows our needs full well. When I think back on my life and consider all the many hours I spent worrying about how we would pay the power bill, buy groceries, purchase new school clothes or something as simple as paying for a field trip, I can truly put verse twenty-six into perspective, "Look at the birds of the air; they do not sow or reap or store away in barns, and yet your heavenly Father feeds them."

Although it seemed He would allow me to worry just a bit, I am always encouraged to simply wait on Him. Sometimes the answer would come in a way unexpected; a rebate check in the morning mail, a friend offering hand-me-downs, or our child offering to give up something to bring about a much needed solution. Those are the times embedded deep in my heart; the times I fell to my knees and asked forgiveness for my inability to trust. Give yourself the opportunity to make each day a day of peace rather than a day of unnecessary worry. The ability is within each of us.

"Who of you by worrying
can add a single hour to his life?"
Matthew 6:27 (NIV ®)

Date _____ Prayer Need _____

_____

Date _____ Prayer Need _____

_____

Date _____ Prayer Need _____

_____

Date _____ Prayer Need _____

_____

Date _____ Prayer Need _____

_____

Date _____ Prayer Need _____

_____

Date _____ Prayer Need _____

_____

Date _____ Prayer Need _____

_____

Date _____ Prayer Need _____

_____

Date _____ Prayer Need _____

_____

DATE _____ PRAYER NEED_____

_____

DATE _____ PRAYER NEED_____

_____

DATE _____ PRAYER NEED_____

_____

DATE _____ PRAYER NEED_____

_____

DATE _____ PRAYER NEED_____

_____

DATE _____ PRAYER NEED_____

_____

DATE _____ PRAYER NEED_____

_____

DATE _____ PRAYER NEED_____

_____

_____

*"But seek first His kingdom and His righteousness,
and all these things will be given to you as well."*
Matthew 6:33 (NIV®)

Date _____ Prayer Need _____

_____

Date _____ Prayer Need _____

_____

Date _____ Prayer Need _____

_____

Date _____ Prayer Need _____

_____

Notes

_____

_____

_____

_____

_____

_____

_____

_____

_____

_____

_____

THE MATERIAL WITNESS

Like many Christian households, we have accumulated numerous bibles; some for simple reading and study; some for a variety of translations. There is the "Open Bible", the "Student Bible", the "New International", the "New American Standard" and the "King James". Of course, this is only to name a few. My husband and I use the "NIV Women's and Men's Devotional Bibles" for church. I use three of them for my writing resources, as well as an on-line bible and a bible dictionary. Although we own them all, we certainly do not use them all on a daily basis, but being surrounded by His word is a comfort to us. We also have numerous framed art pieces, scriptures and plaques throughout our home that represent and solidify our walk with Christ; not just to others, but to ourselves, as well. It is comforting when friends or family come to visit and these possessions assist us in our witness that Christ is the foundation and center of our home.

Of course, a few bibles, framed scriptures and the Serenity Prayer displayed on the wall do not define whether Christ resides in the heart of an individual. It is our actions, words, devotion and steadfastness in our daily walk that prove this to be true. Demonstrate your love of the Father to everyone you meet, your co-workers, your family and your friends. Allow His Spirit in you to reflect through your life to others.

"Come, follow Me," Jesus said,
"And I will make you fishers of men."
Mark 1:17 (NIV®)

Date _____ Prayer Need _____

_____

Date _____ Prayer Need _____

_____

Date _____ Prayer Need _____

_____

Date _____ Prayer Need _____

_____

Date _____ Prayer Need _____

_____

Date _____ Prayer Need _____

_____

Date _____ Prayer Need _____

_____

Date _____ Prayer Need _____

_____

Date _____ Prayer Need _____

_____

Date _____ Prayer Need _____

_____

DATE _____ PRAYER NEED _____

_____

_____

DATE _____ PRAYER NEED _____

_____

_____

DATE _____ PRAYER NEED _____

_____

_____

DATE _____ PRAYER NEED _____

_____

_____

DATE _____ PRAYER NEED _____

_____

_____

DATE _____ PRAYER NEED _____

_____

_____

DATE _____ PRAYER NEED _____

_____

_____

DATE _____ PRAYER NEED _____

_____

_____

"... faith comes from hearing the message,
and the message is heard through the word of Christ."
Romans 10:17 (NIV R)

DATE _____ PRAYER NEED _____

_____

DATE _____ PRAYER NEED _____

_____

DATE _____ PRAYER NEED _____

_____

DATE _____ PRAYER NEED _____

_____

NOTES

_____

_____

_____

_____

_____

_____

_____

_____

_____

_____

_____

A Time for Fresh Faith †

Once again, the day has come to say, "I am on my knees for me." Time to take a breath; time to replenish your spiritual strength; time to seek His guidance and to petition the Lord for yourself; time to ask Him for a refreshing of your spirit.

On the reverse of this page, list the areas in your own life where you desire His help; financial, physical, spiritual, or emotional.

Be willing to remove your shoes and lay face down before Him. He adores you and wants your desires to become His.

Open your heart, call out His name …
Allow Him to offer "Fresh Faith."

"Delight yourself in the Lord
and He will give you the desires of your heart.
Commit your way to the Lord; trust in Him and He will do this:
He will make your righteousness shine like the dawn,
the justice of your cause like the noonday sun."
Psalms 37:4-6 (NIV ®)

MY PRAYER, MY NEEDS

"Do not be anxious about anything, but in everything,
by prayer and petition, with thanksgiving,
present your requests to God .
And the peace of God, which transcends all understanding,
will guard your hearts and your minds in Christ Jesus."
Philippians 4:6-7 (NIV®)

WORTH THE WAIT

In my senior year of high school, I took a writing class to fill in an elective and complete my second semester requirements. We were to write a one thousand word essay detailing our view of life after graduation. This task would prove to be a simple one, as I was already engaged to my high school sweetheart, who was currently serving in the U.S. Navy and my future was already in place. I envisioned our home, children, and a dedicated husband and father. What I did not envision was any religious affiliation. This was not a part of my life nor was it a part of his. Not then or even when we exchanged vows one year later. It was not until five years of marriage that we found the missing piece in our relationship. Someone had been praying for us; praying that we would realize the absence of Christ in our home and the absence of true mercy, grace, and forgiveness. That someone was my mother-in-law.

The night we accepted Him into our lives and into our future, my husband made the call that Mom had been longing for. Choking back tears, he told her of our life changing commitment to serve Him. As they wept together, our lives began to take on new meaning. She had been praying for her son for twenty-six years. Patience and persistence, love and hope all have their rewards. Continue to pray for the lost … this is our calling, no matter how long the wait.

"Wait for the Lord;
be strong and take heart and wait for the Lord"
Psalm 27:14 (NIV®)

Date _____ Prayer Need _____
_____

Date _____ Prayer Need _____
_____

Date _____ Prayer Need _____
_____

Date _____ Prayer Need _____
_____

Date _____ Prayer Need _____
_____

Date _____ Prayer Need _____
_____

Date _____ Prayer Need _____
_____

Date _____ Prayer Need _____
_____

Date _____ Prayer Need _____
_____

Date _____ Prayer Need _____
_____

DATE _____ PRAYER NEED _____

_____

DATE _____ PRAYER NEED _____

_____

DATE _____ PRAYER NEED _____

_____

DATE _____ PRAYER NEED _____

_____

DATE _____ PRAYER NEED _____

_____

DATE _____ PRAYER NEED _____

_____

DATE _____ PRAYER NEED _____

_____

DATE _____ PRAYER NEED _____

_____

_____

"In that day they will say, 'Surely this is our God;
we trusted in Him and He saved us.
This is the Lord, we trusted in Him;
let us rejoice and be glad in His salvation.'"
Isaiah 25:9 (NIV/R)

Date _____ Prayer Need _____

_____

Date _____ Prayer Need _____

_____

Date _____ Prayer Need _____

_____

Date _____ Prayer Need _____

_____

_____

NOTES

_____

_____

_____

_____

_____

_____

_____

_____

_____

_____

_____

It's All Good

Giving thanks to the Father is a simple task. There is so much in my life, actually every single aspect of my life that I should give Him thanks for. Truly, if I tried to thank Him for everything I would be on my knees forever. The good things, the bad things that made me thankful for the good things, and the missed opportunities all brought some purpose and meaning to, again … the good things. As parents, we spend a great deal of time teaching our children manners. Saying "please" and "thank you" are the first attempts at this parental task. I can still hear my daughters repeating "pease" and "tattoo" as toddlers. Regardless, they did learn and they are passing on the same "good" manners to our grandchildren.

We also taught them to pray. Included in those prayers was the early understanding of thanking God for the good things like mommy, daddy and Jesus; things yet to come like a new day and new friends; and for His forgiveness for the not so good things; like telling a fib, arguing, or not doing their homework, because the reprimand taught them a lesson not to repeat! So, pray without ceasing. Give Him honor and thanks for all areas of your life … the good and the not so good.

"O' give thanks to the Lord, for He is good;
His love endures forever."
1 Chronicles 16:34 (NIV R)

Date _____ Prayer Need_____
_____

Date _____ Prayer Need_____
_____

Date _____ Prayer Need_____
_____

Date _____ Prayer Need_____
_____

Date _____ Prayer Need_____
_____

Date _____ Prayer Need_____
_____

Date _____ Prayer Need_____
_____

Date _____ Prayer Need_____
_____

Date _____ Prayer Need_____
_____

Date _____ Prayer Need_____
_____

DATE _____PRAYER NEED_____

_____

_____

DATE _____PRAYER NEED_____

_____

_____

DATE _____PRAYER NEED_____

_____

_____

DATE _____PRAYER NEED_____

_____

_____

DATE _____PRAYER NEED_____

_____

_____

DATE _____PRAYER NEED_____

_____

_____

DATE _____PRAYER NEED_____

_____

_____

DATE _____PRAYER NEED_____

_____

_____

"...Always giving thanks to God the Father for everything,
in the name of the Lord Jesus Christ"
Ephesians 5:20 (NIV®)

DATE _____ PRAYER NEED _____

_____

_____

DATE _____ PRAYER NEED _____

_____

_____

DATE _____ PRAYER NEED _____

_____

_____

DATE _____ PRAYER NEED _____

_____

_____

NOTES

_____

_____

_____

_____

_____

_____

_____

_____

_____

_____

_____

_____

A Minute to Live It

There is a popular game show where contestants use household items to complete a task with only a single minute on the clock. The ultimate goal is to accomplish each challenge in an effort to reach the million dollar prize.

When God placed each of us on this earth, He presented a task of choice to complete in order to reach the ultimate prize, "eternal life." That single "task" is described in John 6:29; Jesus replied to the crowd, saying, "The work of God is this: to believe in the One He has sent." It is vital that we consistently put our faith in Christ and the finished work He completed on Calvary. Once we leave the old behind us and choose to begin a new life with Christ, there are essential "tasks" that surface as we mature as Christians. We must _Worship_ by focusing only on Him; _Pray_ by spending time with Him daily; _Repent_ by confessing our sins to the Father each day; stay _Disciplined_ and accountable as we remain in this worldly environment; _Study_ in the word for our spiritual growth; perform _Service_ to others; and, finally, practice _Evangelism_, remembering that Jesus commanded His disciples to spread His message to the world.

My life, as a child of God, is filled with responsibilities. Most importantly, I will follow His greatest commandment, to love Him and to love others. It would take a mere minute of prayer to open your heart to Him, but in doing so, you will have won the ultimate prize … not a million dollars, but a life changing gift of immeasurable value.

*"Love the Lord your God with all your heart and with
all your soul and with all your strength."*
Deuteronomy 6:5 (NIV®)

Date _____ Prayer Need _____
_____

Date _____ Prayer Need _____
_____

Date _____ Prayer Need _____
_____

Date _____ Prayer Need _____
_____

Date _____ Prayer Need _____
_____

Date _____ Prayer Need _____
_____

Date _____ Prayer Need _____
_____

Date _____ Prayer Need _____
_____

Date _____ Prayer Need _____
_____

Date _____ Prayer Need _____
_____

DATE _____ PRAYER NEED _____

_____

DATE _____ PRAYER NEED _____

_____

DATE _____ PRAYER NEED _____

_____

DATE _____ PRAYER NEED _____

_____

DATE _____ PRAYER NEED _____

_____

DATE _____ PRAYER NEED _____

_____

DATE _____ PRAYER NEED _____

_____

DATE _____ PRAYER NEED _____

_____

_____

"This is what the Lord says: 'Stand at the crossroads and look;
ask for the ancient paths, ask where the good way is, and walk in it,
and you will find rest for your souls ... '"
Jeremiah 6:16 (NIV®)

DATE _____ PRAYER NEED _____
_____

DATE _____ PRAYER NEED _____
_____

DATE _____ PRAYER NEED _____
_____

DATE _____ PRAYER NEED _____
_____
_____

NOTES

_____
_____
_____
_____
_____
_____
_____
_____
_____
_____
_____

A Mother's Voice

Our fifteen year old granddaughter, MaKaylee, will often ask to sleepover. Our grandchildren grow so quickly that we take every opportunity to spend time together. Last year, at fourteen, she was making the transition from middle school to high school and was experiencing an equitable amount of anxiety. When she asked to spend the weekend we welcomed the chance to spend time with her.

That evening, while dressing for bed, she exhibited a mannerism that simply was not our Kaylee. After all, she was fourteen and teenagers house their own form of expression; however, this was perplexing. I sat on the side of the bed and offered to pray with her. She smiled softly and closed her eyes. I prayed allowed and she responded with a soft "amen" when I was finished. I asked her if she would like me to sit with her a while. She began to cry, ever so softly, but as the tears rolled down both cheeks, she confessed. She missed her mom and she always prayed with her mom before bed. I was pleased to know the solution was simple. I promptly called my daughter and placed the phone in MaKaylee's hand. They prayed together then spoke for a moment, exchanging "I love yous." She handed me the phone, wiped her tears, gave me a bigger than normal hug, laid her head on the pillow and closed her eyes. I kissed her on the forehead and thanked Jesus for her sweet spirit. It took only the words of a mother with a prayer to the Father to calm her heart and bring her peace.

"Children's children are a crown to the aged,
and parents are the pride of their children."
Proverbs 17:6 (NIV ®)

DATE _____ PRAYER NEED_____

_____

DATE _____ PRAYER NEED_____

_____

DATE _____ PRAYER NEED_____

_____

DATE _____ PRAYER NEED_____

_____

DATE _____ PRAYER NEED_____

_____

DATE _____ PRAYER NEED_____

_____

DATE _____ PRAYER NEED_____

_____

DATE _____ PRAYER NEED_____

_____

DATE _____ PRAYER NEED_____

_____

DATE _____ PRAYER NEED_____

_____

DATE _____ PRAYER NEED_____
_____
_____

DATE _____ PRAYER NEED_____
_____

DATE _____ PRAYER NEED_____
_____

DATE _____ PRAYER NEED_____
_____

DATE _____ PRAYER NEED_____
_____

DATE _____ PRAYER NEED_____
_____

DATE _____ PRAYER NEED_____
_____

DATE _____ PRAYER NEED_____
_____
_____

*"But from everlasting to everlasting
the Lord's love is with those who fear Him, and His righteousness
with their children's children—with those who keep His covenant
and remember to obey His precepts"*
Psalm 103:17-18 (NIV®)

Date _____ Prayer Need _____
_____

Date _____ Prayer Need _____
_____

Date _____ Prayer Need _____
_____

Date _____ Prayer Need _____
_____

Notes

_____
_____
_____
_____
_____
_____
_____
_____
_____
_____

A Time for Fresh Faith †

Once again, the day has come to say, "I am on my knees for me." Time to take a breath; time to replenish your spiritual strength; time to seek His guidance and to petition the Lord for yourself; time to ask Him for a refreshing of your spirit.

On the reverse of this page, list the areas in your own life where you desire His help; financial, physical, spiritual, or emotional.

Be willing to remove your shoes and lay face down before Him. He adores you and wants your desires to become His.

Open your heart, call out His name …
Allow Him to offer "Fresh Faith."

*"Delight yourself in the Lord
and He will give you the desires of your heart.
Commit your way to the Lord; trust in Him and He will do this:
He will make your righteousness shine like the dawn,
the justice of your cause like the noonday sun."
Psalms 37:4-6* (NIV R)

My Prayer, My Needs

_____

_____

_____

_____

_____

_____

_____

_____

_____

_____

_____

_____

_____

_____

_____

_____

_____

"Do not be anxious about anything, but in everything,
by prayer and petition, with thanksgiving,
present your requests to God .
And the peace of God, which transcends all understanding,
will guard your hearts and your minds in Christ Jesus."
Philippians 4:6-7 (NIV®)

An Eye-Opener

Sometimes our learning experiences are by chance and sometimes we innocently create them ourselves. Dad was extremely proficient in so many areas of his life; a remarkable inventor, a skilled machinist, and a successful businessman. He was also a meticulously organized individual. On a lazy Saturday afternoon, he had decided to tidy up in the garage. Having purchased several cases of motor oil the previous day, he set out to find the perfect storage location to enable easy access. He set the cases on his workbench and, using a pocket knife, cut a can sized hole in the front of one of the boxes. A simple solution for quick retrieval and still having the convenient use of the box to keep them contained. Stacking the remaining two cases in a storage cabinet, he turned his attention to the box he had altered. He had elected to place it on top of an oversized, upright freezer. Lifting the box overhead, his error in calculation suddenly came into full view as the first can, resting directly in the opening, came tumbling out. His "Mechanic's Pocketbook of Tables, Rules, and Formulas" couldn't help him this time! As the unrestrained, single culprit hit him square between the eyes, Mom could clearly hear his audible "frustration," keeping her distance in the kitchen.

Often the life lessons we learn are discovered by witnessing the mistakes of others or even experiencing our own. In Psalm 119:33, David wrote, "God, teach me lessons for living, so I may stay the course." God allows mistakes, but *we* must choose to learn from them.

"Whatever you do, work at it with all your heart,
as working for the Lord, not for men."
Colossians 3:23 (NIV®)

DATE _____ PRAYER NEED _____

_____

DATE _____ PRAYER NEED _____

_____

DATE _____ PRAYER NEED _____

_____

DATE _____ PRAYER NEED _____

_____

DATE _____ PRAYER NEED _____

_____

DATE _____ PRAYER NEED _____

_____

DATE _____ PRAYER NEED _____

_____

DATE _____ PRAYER NEED _____

_____

DATE _____ PRAYER NEED _____

_____

DATE _____ PRAYER NEED _____

_____

DATE _____ PRAYER NEED _____
_____
_____

DATE _____ PRAYER NEED _____
_____
_____

DATE _____ PRAYER NEED _____
_____
_____

DATE _____ PRAYER NEED _____
_____
_____

DATE _____ PRAYER NEED _____
_____
_____

DATE _____ PRAYER NEED _____
_____
_____

DATE _____ PRAYER NEED _____
_____
_____

DATE _____ PRAYER NEED _____
_____
_____

"Like an earring of gold or an ornament of fine gold
is a wise man's rebuke to a listening ear."
Proverbs 25:12 (NIV®)

DATE _____ PRAYER NEED _____

_____

DATE _____ PRAYER NEED _____

_____

DATE _____ PRAYER NEED _____

_____

DATE _____ PRAYER NEED _____

_____

NOTES

_____

_____

_____

_____

_____

_____

_____

_____

_____

_____

FALLING FROM GRACE

Christ sees our heart inside and out. Living for Him and proving our continued devotion is more than attending church, adding to the collection plate, volunteering to teach Sunday school or offering a meal to a bedridden neighbor. Living the life of a Christian means doing these things because of our dedication to Christ. Churches are full of believers and, yes, unbelievers. Some walk the fence without making a decision to follow Him. Some have made a past decision and choose only to *show* others they are Christians as defined by this world, but fail to truly *live* their decision as defined by Christ. Our calling is to allow the Savior to radiate through us; to lift our hands in praise without awkwardness; to offer prayer without inhibition; to shed tears without embarrassment.

My heart tells me this ... knowing Him, but not sharing Him would be a sad and regretful circumstance, as though I had never met Him at all. Going from day to day; never sharing His love, His mercy, and His forgiveness would be a sorrowful existence. We must all continue to remember ... we possess this eternal gift in our heart, because of the compassion of an individual, stranger or otherwise, who extended a hand to us with an offer of prayer for salvation.

"Your attitude should be the same as that of Christ Jesus...
but made himself nothing, taking the very nature of a servant,
being made in human likeness.
Philippians 2:5& 7 (NIV®)

DATE _____ PRAYER NEED _____
_____

DATE _____ PRAYER NEED _____
_____

DATE _____ PRAYER NEED _____
_____

DATE _____ PRAYER NEED _____
_____

DATE _____ PRAYER NEED _____
_____

DATE _____ PRAYER NEED _____
_____

DATE _____ PRAYER NEED _____
_____

DATE _____ PRAYER NEED _____
_____

DATE _____ PRAYER NEED _____
_____

DATE _____ PRAYER NEED _____
_____

DATE _____ PRAYER NEED _____

_____

DATE _____ PRAYER NEED _____

_____

DATE _____ PRAYER NEED _____

_____

DATE _____ PRAYER NEED _____

_____

DATE _____ PRAYER NEED _____

_____

DATE _____ PRAYER NEED _____

_____

DATE _____ PRAYER NEED _____

_____

DATE _____ PRAYER NEED _____

_____

"Be joyful in hope, patient in affliction, faithful in prayer.
Share with God's people who are in need.
Practice hospitality."
Romans 12:12-13 (NIV®)

DATE _____ PRAYER NEED _____

_____

DATE _____ PRAYER NEED _____

_____

DATE _____ PRAYER NEED _____

_____

DATE _____ PRAYER NEED _____

_____

_____

NOTES

_____

_____

_____

_____

_____

_____

_____

_____

_____

_____

_____

A Profitable Trade

I don't believe I have ever met anyone who can say they have no regrets; no regrets for past decisions, no regrets for past relationships, no regrets for past circumstances. Every decision, every relationship, and every circumstance in our past; good or bad, has spilled into our present life. Good decisions are always welcome ones. They may have allowed us to pass blessings to others. Regretful decisions are something altogether different. Imagine having to physically carry around a ten pound boulder. You cannot set it down, no one else can hold it or carry it for you and it goes with you no matter your destination. We are so blessed to have a Savior who will gladly take that burden from us.

Now … close your eyes and imagine gently handing that burden of past sins and regretful decisions to Him. Do you feel that? The weight is lifted; your arms drop to your sides; your soul cries out in relief.

Our Father offers each of us the opportunity to hand Him our past regrets. They have no place in this new life. We cannot change the past, but we can enrich the future. He is our Source and He offers forgiveness for all our past transgressions. Give them up … run to Him.

"In Him we have redemption through His blood,
the forgiveness of sins,
in accordance with the riches of God's grace
that He lavished on us with all wisdom and understanding."
Ephesians 1:7 (NIV®)

DATE _____ PRAYER NEED _____
_____

DATE _____ PRAYER NEED _____
_____

DATE _____ PRAYER NEED _____
_____

DATE _____ PRAYER NEED _____
_____

DATE _____ PRAYER NEED _____
_____

DATE _____ PRAYER NEED _____
_____

DATE _____ PRAYER NEED _____
_____

DATE _____ PRAYER NEED _____
_____

DATE _____ PRAYER NEED _____
_____

DATE _____ PRAYER NEED _____
_____

DATE _____ PRAYER NEED_____

_____

DATE _____ PRAYER NEED_____

_____

DATE _____ PRAYER NEED_____

_____

DATE _____ PRAYER NEED_____

_____

DATE _____ PRAYER NEED_____

_____

DATE _____ PRAYER NEED_____

_____

DATE _____ PRAYER NEED_____

_____

DATE _____ PRAYER NEED_____

_____

_____

"...and do not give the devil a foothold."
Ephesians 4:27 (NIV®)

DATE _____ PRAYER NEED _____

_____

DATE _____ PRAYER NEED _____

_____

DATE _____ PRAYER NEED _____

_____

DATE _____ PRAYER NEED _____

_____

NOTES

_____

_____

_____

_____

_____

_____

_____

_____

_____

_____

_____

_____

I DREAM

To aspire, to hope, to desire; all are a quest in which we forge ahead to create a reality; fulfilling our most desired dreams. I remember, as a child, my dreams were nowhere near my adult interpretation. My hopes were in being a teacher or a nurse. However, I did fulfill both my childhood aspirations when I became a mom; both teacher and nurse. Of course, I also aspired as a chauffeur, a seamstress, a counselor, a hair stylist, a financial advisor, a professional shopper, and a jailer (so my daughter's would agree); none of which were on my list, but certainly could fill up a resume.

Believing in ourselves and our aspirations can be a very challenging task. I have always wanted to write, to share my stories; my thoughts; my faith with others. It has always been a dream. It was something I saw no reality in and found no ability to make it happen. It took more than twenty-five years, but I am actually living my passion. Granted, the circumstances were not as I would have hoped for or expected, but still, the plan was there all along. I want to offer hope and the belief that dreams can come true. They don't always come in the manner we expect, but trust His plan for you. Our Father knows the desires of your heart and longs to help you fulfill your dreams.

"Trust in the Lord, and do good; dwell in the land and enjoy safe pasture. Delight yourself in the Lord and He will give you the desires of your heart."
Psalm 37:3-4 (NIV ®)

DATE _____ PRAYER NEED _____
_____

DATE _____ PRAYER NEED _____
_____

DATE _____ PRAYER NEED _____
_____

DATE _____ PRAYER NEED _____
_____

DATE _____ PRAYER NEED _____
_____

DATE _____ PRAYER NEED _____
_____

DATE _____ PRAYER NEED _____
_____

DATE _____ PRAYER NEED _____
_____

DATE _____ PRAYER NEED _____
_____

DATE _____ PRAYER NEED _____
_____

DATE _____ PRAYER NEED _____
_____
_____

DATE _____ PRAYER NEED _____
_____
_____

DATE _____ PRAYER NEED _____
_____
_____

DATE _____ PRAYER NEED _____
_____
_____

DATE _____ PRAYER NEED _____
_____
_____

DATE _____ PRAYER NEED _____
_____
_____

DATE _____ PRAYER NEED _____
_____
_____

DATE _____ PRAYER NEED _____
_____
_____

"Again, I tell you ,
that if two of you on earth agree about anything you ask for,
It will be done for you by My Father in heaven."
Matthew 18:19 (NIV®)

Date _____ Prayer Need _____
_____
_____

Date _____ Prayer Need _____
_____
_____

Date _____ Prayer Need _____
_____
_____

Date _____ Prayer Need _____
_____
_____

NOTES

_____
_____
_____
_____
_____
_____
_____
_____
_____
_____
_____

A Time for Fresh Faith †

Once again, the day has come to say, "I am on my knees for me." Time to take a breath; time to replenish your spiritual strength; time to seek His guidance and to petition the Lord for yourself; time to ask Him for a refreshing of your spirit.

On the reverse of this page, list the areas in your own life where you desire His help; financial, physical, spiritual, or emotional.

Be willing to remove your shoes and lay face down before Him. He adores you and wants your desires to become His.

Open your heart, call out His name …
Allow Him to offer "Fresh Faith."

"Delight yourself in the Lord
and He will give you the desires of your heart.
Commit your way to the Lord; trust in Him and He will do this:
He will make your righteousness shine like the dawn,
the justice of your cause like the noonday sun."
Psalms 37:4-6 (NIV®)

My Prayer, My Needs

"Do not be anxious about anything, but in everything,
by prayer and petition, with thanksgiving,
present your requests to God.
And the peace of God, which transcends all understanding,
will guard your hearts and your minds in Christ Jesus."
Philippians 4:6-7 (NIV®)

Joy Everlasting

On a wall in my living room hangs a two foot by three foot, metal art piece. In the center, in eight inch letters, it states, simply, "Joy." Just below the word "Joy," is a verse from the book of Luke, chapter six, "Rejoice in that day and leap for joy, because great is your reward in heaven." Pressed into the metal and repeated around the parameter are the words, "Every day is a Gift."

Here's how I see it—it does not matter what circumstances may bring; today, tomorrow or the next day. The message is clear. Every day is its own gift. Yesterday is gone and today declares a new start. God awakens us to each new day. Rejoice in it and thank Him for it. Breathe in a new gift of life, a gift of a new beginning, a gift that offers us a fresh start; perhaps to meet a new friend, reconcile a lost relationship, spend a day with family, or curl up in your easy chair with a good book. We may have days ahead that will hold laughter, surprise, pain or even sadness; we may use the day to complete a task or to do absolutely nothing, but by viewing each day as a new start, it will always be His perfect gift.

"This is the day the Lord has made;
let us rejoice and be glad in it."
Psalm 118:24 (NIV®)

Date _____ Prayer Need _____
_____

Date _____ Prayer Need _____
_____

Date _____ Prayer Need _____
_____

Date _____ Prayer Need _____
_____

Date _____ Prayer Need _____
_____

Date _____ Prayer Need _____
_____

Date _____ Prayer Need _____
_____

Date _____ Prayer Need _____
_____

Date _____ Prayer Need _____
_____

Date _____ Prayer Need _____
_____

DATE _____ PRAYER NEED _____

_____

_____

DATE _____ PRAYER NEED _____

_____

_____

DATE _____ PRAYER NEED _____

_____

_____

DATE _____ PRAYER NEED _____

_____

_____

DATE _____ PRAYER NEED _____

_____

_____

DATE _____ PRAYER NEED _____

_____

_____

DATE _____ PRAYER NEED _____

_____

_____

DATE _____ PRAYER NEED _____

_____

_____

"Rejoice in that day and leap for JOY,
because great is your reward in heaven ... "
Luke 6:23 (NIV/R)

DATE _____ PRAYER NEED _____

_____

DATE _____ PRAYER NEED _____

_____

DATE _____ PRAYER NEED _____

_____

DATE _____ PRAYER NEED _____

_____

NOTES

_____

_____

_____

_____

_____

_____

_____

_____

_____

_____

_____

THE ETERNAL GIFT

As a grandparent, not many events parallel the news of a grandchild having given their heart to Jesus. Today, my granddaughter, MaKaylee, returned from senior high church camp in Pendleton, OR. MaKaylee and her mom stopped by while I was caring for our twin granddaughters. As soon as I saw her face, I knew there was a change in her life and in her heart. She had given her life to Him nearly nine years earlier, but a surrendered life at the age of six can hold many challenges. Now, at fifteen, she has found a renewed heart and a Savior who has been patient; allowing her to come to Him, once again, on her knees … in her time. Her life is whole and the joy in her face tells the entire story.

MaKaylee is an amazing young lady. She stands on the promise of God's word and is filled with joy and abundant love. I am embarrassed to say that listening to her experience and hearing the joy and excitement in her voice, sparks a tiny bit of envy. Oh how I would love to have had the same opportunities at the impressionable age of fifteen; to be able to tell everyone that I have a Savior who loves me and to share His mercy and forgiveness. Today, the Lord gave me a gift. Thanking Him is not nearly enough.

Live each day as though it were the first day you prayed for salvation; the day you received His ultimate gift. He is truly a gift that keeps on giving; no matter how many times you ask!

"For Lord is good and His love endures forever;
His faithfulness continues through all generations."
Psalm 100:5 (NIV R)

Date _____ Prayer Need _____

_____

Date _____ Prayer Need _____

_____

Date _____ Prayer Need _____

_____

Date _____ Prayer Need _____

_____

Date _____ Prayer Need _____

_____

Date _____ Prayer Need _____

_____

Date _____ Prayer Need _____

_____

Date _____ Prayer Need _____

_____

Date _____ Prayer Need _____

_____

Date _____ Prayer Need _____

_____

DATE _____ PRAYER NEED _____

_____

_____

DATE _____ PRAYER NEED _____

_____

_____

DATE _____ PRAYER NEED _____

_____

_____

DATE _____ PRAYER NEED _____

_____

_____

DATE _____ PRAYER NEED _____

_____

_____

DATE _____ PRAYER NEED _____

_____

_____

DATE _____ PRAYER NEED _____

_____

_____

DATE _____ PRAYER NEED _____

_____

_____

"Sing to the Lord a new song,
for He has done marvelous things;
His right hand and His holy arm
have worked salvation for Him."
Psalm 98:1 (NIV®)

Date _____ Prayer Need_____

_____

Date _____ Prayer Need_____

_____

Date _____ Prayer Need_____

_____

Date _____ Prayer Need_____

_____

_____

Notes

_____

_____

_____

_____

_____

_____

_____

_____

_____

_____

_____

A Sweet Harvest

Paul writes to us in Galatians, chapter five, "Live by the Spirit and you will not gratify the desires of the sinful nature. For the sinful nature desires what is contrary to the Spirit and the Spirit, what is contrary to the sinful nature."

We must fill our lives with "Spiritual Fruit;" love, joy, peace, patience, kindness, goodness, faithfulness, gentleness and self-control. These are the qualities of a true Christian life. God is aware that we are human and not one of us is perfect, but God calls us to strive for perfection and the qualities that Paul has listed. The Holy Spirit remains with us on earth to guide us; to teach us to be Christ like; to bring us closer to Him. We must change our earthly ways towards others and within ourselves.

We each have a "Spiritual Fruit Bowl." Continue to strive in filling it to overflowing with the qualities that the Spirit is offering to teach you; qualities that are freely given. Trust that the Spirit will work within you to make the changes that God desires to perfect. It is the attributes the Holy Spirit brings, that will allow others to see Christ through you.

"But the fruit of the Spirit is love, joy, peace,
patience, kindness, goodness,
faithfulness, gentleness and self-control.
Against such things there is no law."
Galatians 5:22 & 23 (NIV ®)

Date _____ Prayer Need _____

_____

Date _____ Prayer Need _____

_____

Date _____ Prayer Need _____

_____

Date _____ Prayer Need _____

_____

Date _____ Prayer Need _____

_____

Date _____ Prayer Need _____

_____

Date _____ Prayer Need _____

_____

Date _____ Prayer Need _____

_____

Date _____ Prayer Need _____

_____

Date _____ Prayer Need _____

_____

DATE _____ PRAYER NEED _____
_____

DATE _____ PRAYER NEED _____
_____

DATE _____ PRAYER NEED _____
_____

DATF _____ PRAYER NEED _____
_____

DATE _____ PRAYER NEED _____
_____

DATE _____ PRAYER NEED _____
_____

DATE _____ PRAYER NEED _____
_____

DATE _____ PRAYER NEED _____
_____
_____

*"Those who belong to Christ Jesus
have crucified the sinful nature
with its passions and desires."*
Galatians 5:24 (NIV®)

Date _____ Prayer Need _____
_____

Date _____ Prayer Need _____
_____

Date _____ Prayer Need _____
_____

Date _____ Prayer Need _____
_____

NOTES

_____
_____
_____
_____
_____
_____
_____
_____
_____
_____
_____
_____

A Final Thought

Sharing personal and intimate stories of my past has opened my eyes even wider to the many blessings in my life and has further fueled my desire to write in Christ's name. "Christ's name," it is a humbling experience to have the privilege of even speaking His name aloud. Consider this … there are more than 100 different names for Jesus found in the Bible. In Deuteronomy, He is our "Rock;" in Psalm, He is "Jehovah;" in Isaiah, He is the "Prince of Peace;" in Jeremiah, He is "Our Comforter;" in Matthew, He is "Teacher;" in Mark, He is the "Son of Mary;" in Luke He is "Savior, the Son of the Most High;" and in John, He is the "Bread of Life," the "Lamb of God," "Messiah …" He is the "Light of the World."

I want to use this last entry to offer encouragement in your walk with Him. If you have already opened your heart to the Savior, take time each day to thank Him for every single blessing He has gifted you; take opportunity to share His grace and mercy with others. Life is a gift; a gift that has been graciously and lovingly given to each of us. But, if you have never made a personal commitment to our Lord and Savior, please know this, when your life includes Him and your heart is completely and overwhelmingly filled with His love, His mercy, and His grace, you will see this world through His compassion; and to know Him is to never be the same again. You need only to ask Him to come into your life, ask Him to forgive you, to lead you, and confess Him as Savior. He will do the rest.

"I write to you, dear children, because your sins
have been forgiven on account of His name."
1 John 2:12 (NIV/R)

Date _____ Prayer Need _____

_____

Date _____ Prayer Need _____

_____

Date _____ Prayer Need _____

_____

Date _____ Prayer Need _____

_____

Date _____ Prayer Need _____

_____

Date _____ Prayer Need _____

_____

Date _____ Prayer Need _____

_____

Date _____ Prayer Need _____

_____

Date _____ Prayer Need _____

_____

Date _____ Prayer Need _____

_____

DATE _____ PRAYER NEED_____

_____

DATE _____ PRAYER NEED_____

_____

DATE _____ PRAYER NEED_____

_____

DATE _____ PRAYER NEED_____

_____

DATE _____ PRAYER NEED_____

_____

DATE _____ PRAYER NEED_____

_____

DATE _____ PRAYER NEED_____

_____

DATE _____ PRAYER NEED_____

_____

"... the same Lord is Lord of all
and richly blesses all who call on Him,
for everyone who calls on the name of the Lord
will be saved."'
Romans 10:12-13 (NIV®)

Date _____ Prayer Need _____

_____

Date _____ Prayer Need _____

_____

Date _____ Prayer Need _____

_____

Date _____ Prayer Need _____

_____

Notes

_____

_____

_____

_____

_____

_____

_____

_____

_____

_____

_____

" We fix our eyes not on what is seen,
but on what is unseen.
For what is seen is temporary,
but what is unseen is eternal."
II Corinthians 4:18 (NIV R)

Though our life

Begins as a gift and

Its ending is pre-planned;

It is the journey

And His mercy

That offer us eternity.

"As the rain and the snow come down from heaven,
and do not return to it without watering the earth
and making it bud and flourish, so that it yields seed
for the sower and bread for the eater,
so is My Word that goes out from my mouth:
It will not return to Me empty,
but will accomplish what I desire
and achieve the purpose for which I sent it."

Isaiah 55:10-11 (NIV®)